Writing the Doctoral Dissertation

A SYSTEMATIC APPROACH

by

GORDON B. DAVIS
Professor, Management Sciences and
Accounting, Graduate School of Business
Administration, University of Minnesota

CLYDE A. PARKER
Professor, Educational Psychology
University of Minnesota

BARRON'S EDUCATIONAL SERIES, INC.
New York • London • Toronto • Sydney

All inquiries should be addressed to:

Barron's Educational Series, Inc.
250 Wireless Boulevard
Hauppauge, New York 11788

Library of Congress Catalog Card No. 78-7598
International Standard Book No. 0-8120-0997-5

Library of Congress Cataloging in Publication Data

Davis, Gordon Bitter.
  Writing the doctoral dissertation.

  Bibliography: p.
  I. Report writing.   2. Dissertations, Academic.
I. Parker, Clyde Alvin, joint author.   II.   Title.
LB2369.D357   808'.042   78-7598
ISBN 0-8120-0997-5

PRINTED IN THE UNITED STATES OF AMERICA
123   510   11 10 9

Contents

Illustrations

Preface

The purpose of this book is to assist doctoral candidates in *completing* a better quality dissertation in a shorter time. Experiences in advising doctoral candidates, in serving on dissertation committees, and in discussions with candidates as they have worked on their dissertations clearly indicate a need for such a book. The approach is also applicable to master's theses, which can be viewed as limited scope dissertations.

This systematic approach assists doctoral candidates in managing the completion of the dissertation task. It also has advantages for the advisor because the method can improve utilization of the scarce faculty resource.

The examples in the text reflect our backgrounds and, therefore, do not attempt to relate to all conditions that students in different fields may face. One might have considerable discussion about the "truth" or appropriateness of the examples or the format of the forms. This would miss the essence. The examples and forms are used to convey, as concretely as possible, the elements of the approach. The essential point is to structure the dissertation project and to manage it to a successful completion. Students and advisors should feel free to modify the approach to reflect advising style and unique subject area and institutional requirements.

This book was begun while Gordon Davis was on leave from the University of Minnesota as a professor of Management at the European Institute for Advanced Studies in Management, Brussels, Belgium. The work of the Institute involved advising a large number of doctoral candidates in the dissertation stage. This experience solidified and improved prior ideas and provided an impetus for the text. The faculty of the Institute reviewed parts of the book and made valuable suggestions that are reflected in the final result. The approach has been presented to doctoral candidates in a number of disciplines at the University of Minnesota and several other universities in the United States. It has also been used by doctoral candidates in foreign countries such as Great Britain, Sweden, Belgium, Germany, and France. The response has been very positive, and the results achieved by candidates as they follow the approach have provided ample evidence of its usefulness.

Comments on the effectiveness of the method and suggestions for improvements in the approach are welcome. They may be sent to either author at the University of Minnesota.

CHAPTER 1

The Need for a Different Approach to the Dissertation

The student taking courses generally operates on a rather short and well-structured time cycle. Assignments are due each class period, papers are due at a fixed time during the term, and examinations are at scheduled times during the term. Research and writing assignments are quite small in scope because they must fit into the framework of a ten-week quarter or a fifteen-week semester. Even fairly large papers are quite well defined in terms of what needs to be done. The period of doctoral dissertation activities is the first time students have been faced with a large, unstructured project, and usually nothing in their prior training has prepared them for managing such a project. This chapter compares the consequences of a traditional, unstructured approach with those from a structured approach. An understanding of these consequences should provide a doctoral candidate with motivation to follow the systematic approach. Although smaller in scope, the master's thesis is a sufficiently large project so that the same problems of noncompletion occur with dismaying frequency. Therefore, master's candidates can apply the case studies to their situation.

Two Case Studies

The following case studies reflect the activities of real students, and illustrate two extremes. One illustrates the consequences of an unmanaged approach, and the other, the advantages of a systematic management approach.

JAMES CARTHLY

James Carthly was a fairly good student. He completed his course work with satisfactory grades and passed the qualifying examinations of the doctoral program. After some time, he selected a dissertation topic area in which he had an interest and began collecting data by an interview method. At the same time, during the early spring, he interviewed to take a position with a university. He seemed to be making good progress in terms of the background and reading, early data collection, and analysis necessary before one can begin to write the dissertation itself. However, he had never prepared a complete dissertation proposal or a plan for completion. His committee was more or less unaware of the scope of the intended dissertation. They had only a general idea based on his oral comments. There were no meetings of the full committee to discuss the dissertation project. Time passed quickly, and when it was the time for him to begin work at the university where he had accepted a position, there was still no comprehensive proposal or outline of the dissertation for the committee. This didn't worry Carthly because he knew that he had been able to work on the dissertation while doing some teaching as a graduate assistant; he thought there would be even more time for dissertation work with the new position because his teaching load would not be high.

However, he did not anticipate the change in status that came with his new position. He was no longer a graduate student but a young professor (without the thesis completed but, nevertheless, a professor). He now had to teach courses which he had not taught before, so there was much preparation. There were committee meetings, students to advise, and university functions in which to participate. There was a new home to buy, move into, and care for. There were new elementary schools to become acquainted with, and a new community to learn about. When Carthly had been a graduate student, living in student housing, his wife had joined the wives of the other graduate students for social activities among themselves. Generally, they agreed that they should forego many normal social functions in order that their husbands might work the long hours necessary to complete their degrees. His wife had formerly handled many family responsibilites alone, but now she wanted his help. She wanted to attend social functions as well.

The day that he passed the qualifying examinations, there had been general rejoicing because now he was almost through. All he had to do was write the "big" paper. Neither he nor his wife was prepared for the scope of the disseration work and the difficulty of completing it. He contributed to this general situation by having no understanding of how long it would take to finish, no plan, and no time schedule. If the subject were broached, he would say, "Well, I'm making good progress. All I have to do is write it up." But months went on with no visible progress on the dissertation.

At the end of the second year, the Dean told Carthly there would be no salary increase because he had not completed the dissertation. No promotion was possible. He began to feel the pressures for completion. He began to work nights and insist that he could not use holidays and vacations for family activities; he must work on the dissertation. After dinner, he would pull out the dissertation and start work. On those nights that he was able to work, he had about four hours. But by the time he got the material arranged, got himself in the proper frame of mind, reviewed what could be done, and brought himself to the point where he could begin work, the actual effective time spent was very low. He was tired and his mind was not alert.

Finally he decided to take part of the summer and return to work at his university, where he could be near his dissertation advisor. The time he spent there, however, was not highly productive. There was no plan or structure that the advisor and he could agree on. The advisor found it difficult to give good guidance. The committee was not called together because there was not sufficient basis for discussion. But they agreed on some general guidelines for the dissertation and on its general scope. The advisor waited for the student to approach him with questions; the student waited for the advisor to contact him. Very little was accomplished.

Returning home, Carthly kept working, but progress was very slow. The dissertation continued to put a strain on family relations. He always felt that he should be working on the dissertation. His wife felt uncomfortable when they took time for social events or holidays because she had the uneasy feeling that he should be at work. There were no salary raises. He received only temporary appointments. If there had been a cutback, he would have been the first to go. In conferences, Carthly solemnly assured his Dean that work on the dissertation was progressing, and that it should be completed in the coming year. He made these same assurances three years in a row.

Finally, Carthly received notice that the five-year limit for completion of the dissertation was about to expire. If he did not complete the dissertation within the coming year, he would be terminated as a doctoral student and would not be allowed to complete a doctoral degree. He made arrangements to spend full time on the dissertation during the coming summer, foregoing all income possibilities. The dissertation advisor estimated that Carthly would also need the entire fall quarter as well. Therefore, Carthly arranged to leave his family at home, went alone to the university town, and worked full time on the thesis. He had to ask for an extension on the time limit from the university. Since he was almost through, they were willing to grant the short extension required. He did less for the dissertation than he had originally intended, but he finally completed it.

TED MAREN

Ted Maren had an intuitive feel for how to manage a doctoral dissertation. He selected the general area of his dissertation quite early and structured much of his course work to provide support for it. The papers he wrote for these courses were, in reality, background investigations for the dissertation. He was able to make contacts with professors who were interested in the area that he intended to research. He was able to discuss research methodology and ideas for research with the professors. Much of his course work was directly related to the dissertation. In the research methodology course, he planned his research design specifically. In a psychology course, he did a paper related to a particular aspect of his research problem. Even though he had not decided upon the exact topic, he knew the general area and was able to work effectively at getting background information, developing a research design, and testing ideas for a possible specific topic.

After passing the qualifying examination, a dissertation committee was appointed. The committee consisted of professors who knew him and were interested in the general area of the proposed dissertation. Maren proceeded to refine the dissertation proposal until the document clearly defined what he intended to do and the contribution to be made by the dissertation. The committee encouraged him as he developed and sharpened the proposal because they could see the progress he was making. The final proposal, clear and concise, was approved. Maren prepared a time schedule he felt was realistic and followed it as closely as possible. Not everything went as planned. There were some delays he didn't expect, but he was able to estimate quite closely the actual time of completion. The dissertation was completed approximately two months later than originally planned, but well within the margin of error that he had allowed.

He did excellent work, and at the dissertation defense, it was clear that the dissertation would be accepted. The committee was very familiar with it. They had all participated actively in the supervision. Faculty at the dissertation defense who had not been part of the committee had no difficulty understanding the dissertation or its contribution.

At the university where he accepted employment, Maren was able to begin work immediately in his full professorial role. He began immediately serving on committees and participating in professional activities. There was no need to decline social activities with the excuse that "I have to work on my dissertation." There was no delay in publication of professional articles and doing additional research. He was able to accumulate the necessary publication and research record to justify promotion on a timely basis. He had learned to enjoy scholarly work, and it was evident that he was well on his way to a productive career.

The Consequences of Delay in Completion

The most serious possible consequence of a delay in completion is that the doctoral dissertation will never be written and the doctorate will never be obtained. Completion of the dissertation is the big hurdle in obtaining the doctorate. Perhaps as high as one-third of doctoral candidates complete course requirements but never complete the dissertation.

The effects of delay in completion are serious even if there is eventual completion. As a consequence of the delay, the candidate's original committee, perhaps even the advisor, may no longer be available. The topic may no longer be timely. Others may have done research which goes beyond or replaces what he or she is doing. An academic or other career is made much less rewarding. Promotion is made difficult or impossible. There are lost opportunities for writing and other research. The constant pressure to work on the dissertation and complete it disturbs the candidate's home life and reduces effectiveness at work. The dissertation was intended to be a demonstration of ability to do research—the first step in a productive research career. Instead, it has discouraged further research because the project was not completed on a timely basis. If the candidate finally does turn in a completed dissertation that is accepted, he or she is likely to have little enthusiasm for doing more individual research.

The Advantages of Planning and Careful Management

The advantages of timely, planned completion may be inferred from the disadvantages of delayed completion. It is possible to expect improved professional opportunities, improved dissertation quality, and greatly increased incentive to further research. In addition, advantages frequently occur related to financial aid.

Students usually need to apply well in advance for financial aid for support of dissertation work. Applications require that the student present a dissertation proposal along with the application. Students without a completion plan frequently do not have a good proposal and, therefore, are unable to apply for the aid. Students seem willing to borrow money and seek other financial aid for the period when they are taking courses, but seem quite reluctant to take financial risks at the dissertation stage. From a logical standpoint, the time that borrowing is most appropriate is for the completion of the dissertation. Everyone who has had to delay completion of the dissertation can attest to the fact that it reduced income, with the effect lasting even beyond the final completion. This suggests that timely completion frequently has a positive financial payoff. A student who is considering borrowing money might well hesitate if there is uncertainty about the dissertation process and sufficient progress has not been made. However, a student who is following a plan for doing the dissertation, has a reasonable time schedule, and has an accepted proposal, can have some confidence that the project will be completed on time. He or she can therefore take the financial risks necessary to complete the dissertation.

The Problem of the First Position

Many students think a dissertation is just a "big paper," and they think they can do it without too much difficulty. They underestimate the time required, and take a position before they are finished. Recruiting for academic positions is frequently done very early in the year. Some students make the commitment for September during the preceding winter. The student who has begun work on a dissertation in January may feel it will be completed by September. However, unless there has been good planning and scheduling of the work, this is likely to be a false hope.

The first step in solving this problem is for the student to follow a systematic plan and establish a firm completion date. The second step is to negotiate a delayed entry into the first position if the dissertation is not completed. When there was faculty shortage, schools frequently encouraged prospective faculty members to come without completing the dissertation. The result was often a faculty with many long-standing members who never completed their doctoral dissertations. Many schools now have pressures to increase their percentage of professors with doctorates. Therefore, schools are interested in the candidate with a completed doctorate.

The student should discuss frankly with a prospective employer the commitment to complete the doctorate before leaving the university. Completion means an approved draft. The final typing, publication, and other requirements, such as the final dissertation defense, can take place after the student is settled in the new position. But even these steps are better handled before the student leaves. If the student raises the subject and expresses a commitment to finish, it is likely that the university, or other employer with whom he or she is negotiating, will agree to a delayed arrival (at the second semester, for example) if there is an inability to complete the dissertation. Generalizations cannot apply to all employers, but based on the experiences of doctoral candidates who have followed this advice, there is an increasing willingness by universities to agree to these conditions. Such negotiation is more likely to succeed if the student is following a systematic plan for completing the dissertation, with a schedule of activities and a realistic time estimate for completion. The only way a student can make reasonably valid statements as to when the dissertation will be finished is by having such a plan. Casual projections almost always underestimate the time required for completion.

The Philosophy of the Systematic Approach

Three proposition underlie the recommendations in the systematic approach to completing a doctoral dissertation.

1. Structuring of the dissertation project can significantly improve performance (by means of topic analyses, proposal documents, plans, schedules, etc., described in the systematic approach).
2. The student has primary responsibility for the management of the doctoral dissertation project.
3. Faculty (advisor and committee) are a scarce resource.

The first proposition implies that the productivity gap between doctoral dissertation work that is managed and the dissertation work that is unmanaged is large. The same theme in a larger context was stated by a well-regarded researcher in management:

> To make knowledge work productive will be the great management task of this century just as to make manual work productive was the great management task of the last century. The gap between knowledge work that is left unmanaged is probably a great deal wider than was the tremendous difference between manual work before and after the introduction of scientific management. [Peter Drucker, *The Age of Discontinuity* (New York: Harper and Row, 1969), page 272.]

The doctoral dissertation is a large undertaking with certain risks regarding completion and acceptance. However, the risk can be substantially reduced and the probabilities of successful and timely completion can be greatly improved by following a systematic approach to the management of the dissertation project. The objective of the approach is to *complete* a good doctoral dissertation in a reasonable time, but there are some other benefits for students successfully following the approach. Students may gain confidence in their ability to structure and manage research. They will probably do better research following the dissertation. As successful candidates become faculty advisors, an improved understanding of research and dissertation management will probably result, and they will become better advisors.

The second proposition places responsibility for dissertation management on the student. This proposition is reasonable because the dissertation is *the* evidence that the doctoral candidate is capable of independently making a contribution to a field of knowledge. Unfortunately, many students are not able to manage the venture well. The doctoral dissertation is often the first large, unstructured project undertaken by a graduate student. The student may have worked closely with the advisor or other faculty members on significant research projects; indeed, in some cases the doctoral research is an extension of such cooperative research. More often, however, the student has not had such experience and is working alone in a nebulous and ambiguous venture. The advisor and committee provide much help, but it is the student's project; the student must take the responsibility for initiation, planning, executing, and writing.

The third proposition recognizes that faculty advisors are a scarce but very important resource for the dissertation project. The advisor serves as a guide, a critic, a facilitator, and an important source of support. If the advisor performs this role well, the frustrations that the student encounters are minimized. It is our observation that some advisors are better able to facilitate the completion of students' dissertations than others. The exact nature and cause of these advisor differences are not known, but the student should recognize that they exist.

The systematic approach assumes a mutual understanding of advisor-student roles. There is a personal, implied contract between the student and the advisor that the advisor will—

- provide guidance;
- respond to the papers given to read within a reasonable time;
- be reasonably consistent in advice;
- protect the student from unreasonable demands;
- assist the student at those times when the voice of a faculty member advocate is necessary;
- generally aid the student in pursuing the dissertation project.

In this relationship, the student doing the dissertation is expected to—

- do what he or she says will be done when promised (or explain why it cannot be done);
- have integrity in research and writing;
- keep in communication;
- prepare documents for comment;
- follow a method of presentation which effectively uses the

advisor's and committee's time;

- be reasonable in making demands on the time of the advisor and the committee;
- be open to suggestions and to advice, but also show initiative.

Advisors have different advising styles. What is appropriate for one might not be quite right for another. However, this dissertation management approach should be useful to all advisors. It should improve the relationship between the student and the advisor and help to raise the quality of the dissertation. Also, the procedures outlined in the text will help minimize problems in advising and maximize the probabilities of success. The techniques provide for good documentation of the dissertation project. This is especially helpful when changes in the advisor or committee occur.

Students may use the approach unwisely, but generally it appears to have advantages for both the advisor and the student. An experienced advisor knows all of the suggestions in the approach. The value of the publication is that it codifies the advice in a single, short manual. Therefore, the new advisor may also find this manual helpful in becoming a good advisor.

The text has been written so that either a candidate may take the initiative in deciding to follow the method, or an advisor may ask a student to obtain the manual and use the approach. In either case, the advisor may wish to specify amendments or differences in style for the student to follow. For example, one advisor may find it very expedient to have the student prepare an agenda for all committee meetings and, after checking with him or her, to distribute the agenda to the committee members. Another faculty member may feel that an agenda is something the advisor should do alone and, therefore, may tell the student that the agenda suggested in the management approach should not be followed.

Summary

The problem is that students either don't complete the doctoral dissertation or take an unduly long time to do it. Many factors compound the problem, such as the need for financial support and the need to make an advance commitment for a position. However, a large part of the difficulty can be traced to the fact that students do not know how to manage a dissertation project. Nothing in their prior experience has adequately prepared them for it. As a result, they misallocate their efforts, delay in structuring the project, and make unrealistic time estimates. These problems prompted the approach described in this manual.

CHAPTER 2

An Overview of the Dissertation Management Approach

Students write a doctoral dissertation because it is required for a doctor of philosophy (Ph.D.) degree, and also for closely related doctorates in education, and other similar fields.[1] Periodically, there are suggestions that a different doctorate be given to those candidates who intend only to be teachers and that the dissertation should not be required for students who do not intend to do research. These suggestions have so far not received significant support. The students themselves sense that such a doctorate, without a doctoral dissertation, would be viewed by their colleagues as a lesser degree. The doctoral dissertation was instituted as a requirement for good reasons. The reasons are more applicable to some students than for others. However, as long as the requirement exists, students should plan to do it well and make the dissertation project beneficial to their careers. While the systematic approach is written in terms of the doctoral dissertation, it requires only a slight shift in emphasis to make it directly applicable to the master's thesis.

---

[1]A few fields such as dentistry, medicine, and law use the term *doctor* in their degrees, but there is no research or thesis requirement comparable to that of the Ph.D.

The Objectives of a Doctoral Dissertation

Although there may be variations in the way different academic programs view the doctoral dissertation, the requirement appears generally aimed at achieving three objectives having to do with demonstrating the competence of the candidate to—

1. do independent research;
2. make a contribution to knowledge with the research;
3. document the research and make it available to the scholarly community (i.e., write the dissertation).

The dissertation is both a documentation of the fact that the candidate has done independent research and of the contribution to knowledge. From the standpoint of the university, there is no demonstrated ability and no contribution from the research unless the dissertation document is written. [2]

The Nature of the Dissertation Task

What is a doctoral dissertation? It is the documentation of independent research which makes a contribution to knowledge. It is not just a bigger "paper" than papers students have written in connection with various courses. The factors of size, independent research, and contribution place the dissertation in a class apart from prior papers.

The median page length for a dissertation is about 225 pages, but page length ranges from under 100 pages to over 600 pages. Based on the data shown in Figure 2-1 from 400 dissertations plus two other samples of 133 (sociology) and 116 (business administration) from 1971-1972, we have estimated a distribution of page lengths for doctoral dissertations (Figure 2-2). Using 225 as the median and assuming a log-normal distribution (see characteristic shape in Figure 2-1), we estimate—

---

[2] References for students who wish to do general reading on the doctorate and the place of the doctoral dissertation can be found in the bibliography.

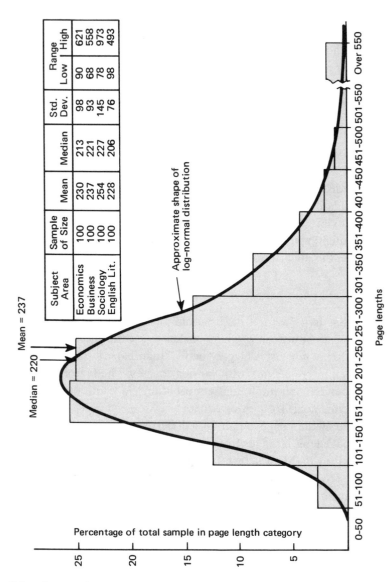

Subject Area	Sample of Size	Mean	Median	Std. Dev.	Range Low	Range High
Economics	100	230	213	98	90	621
Business	100	237	221	93	68	558
Sociology	100	254	227	145	78	973
English Lit.	100	228	206	76	98	493

Approximate shape of log-normal distribution

Mean = 237

Median = 220

Percentage of total sample in page length category

Page lengths

0-50 51-100 101-150 151-200 201-250 251-300 301-350 351-400 401-450 451-500 501-550 Over 550

25 20 15 10 5

2-1. Length Distribution of page for doctoral dissertations in Social Sciences and humanities (sample of 400 dissertations from *Dissertations Abstracts International*, November and December, 1976.)

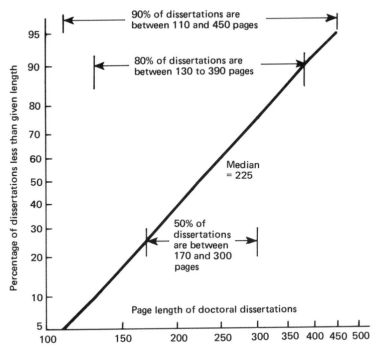

2-2. Estimated page lengths of doctoral dissertations plotted on log-normal graph paper.

- 50 percent of dissertations are from 170 to 300 pages;
- 80 percent of dissertations are from 130 to 390 pages;
- 90 percent of dissertations are from 110 to 450 pages;

It is more difficult to estimate time spent on dissertations. Using a log-normal distribution, we estimate that actual, effective time (actual working hours) for doing a doctoral dissertation from start to finish is about fourteen work months (2,450 hours). Based on distribution in Figure 2-3, we estimate—

- 50 percent of dissertations take from 12½ to 17 work months;
- 80 percent of dissertations require 11 to 19 work months;

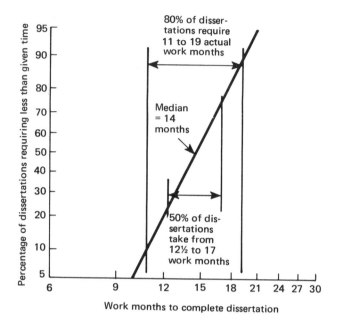

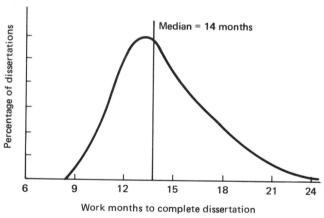

2-3. Estimated actual work months from start of topic search to completed draft of doctoral dissertation (author's estimates).

- 5 percent of dissertations require 10 or less work months;
- 5 percent of dissertations require 21 or more work months.

It should be noted that, unlike the page estimates which are based on an analysis of actual dissertation page lengths, the estimates in Figure 2-3 are rough estimates based on observations of student performance. There appear to be differences in time spent on dissertations related to the field of study, but these are not well documented.

The time estimates represent actual, effective work hours devoted and not the elapsed time during which the candidate worked on the project. The elapsed time over which the work is performed is generally more than one year, say in the neighborhood of one-and-a-half, to three years. Many students take five or more years to complete the dissertation. Some universities have a rule that dissertations must be completed within a certain time (for example, five years) after the qualifying examination has been passed. But other universities establish no cutoff and students still claim to be working on dissertations ten or more years after they have completed all work but the dissertation.

The size of the dissertation makes it substantially different from any paper the student has ever done. It is also unstructured. Up to the point of the dissertation the student has lived in a highly structured environment. Professors who formerly told him or her what to do and how to do it now act as if the student knows what to do. They say, "It's your dissertation. What do you want to do? How do you want to approach the problem? What methodology are you going to use?"

A key element in the dissertation is the contribution the dissertation makes. It is difficult to express what is meant by contribution to knowledge. However, the concept is explored in more detail in Chapter 5.

The question of how good a dissertation should be is difficult to answer. There are good students who never complete the dissertation because they view it as requiring such high quality that they can never achieve what they feel is necessary. The student should probably take a reasonable attitude toward the quality of the doctoral dissertation. One should do a good job as a beginning step in a career, but should not view it as his or her magnum opus. It is unlikely that a dissertation will be the highlight of a student's career because it is done at the beginning of the scholarly career, not at the height. There are a few examples of scholars who have made their major contribution with the doctoral dissertation, but this is not normally so.

In summary, the dissertation task is to carry out a research project which contributes to knowledge and to document the project and its contribution in a written document. The scope of the project can vary, but a typical doctoral dissertation project will require 14 work months, and the documentation will average a length of 225 pages.

The Life Cycle of a Dissertation Project

The dissertation project represents a process of reducing uncertainty. The student begins with the notion of doing research in a broad area of investigation in which there might be thousands of dissertation possibilities. The student must reduce the uncertainty by reducing the number of possibilities he or she is going to consider. This is done by looking closely at several topics and making an evaluation of each. One of the topics is selected and then further defined by the dissertation proposal. Uncertainty is again reduced when a detailed chapter outline is prepared. Uncertainty is eliminated when the research has been done, the text of the dissertation has been written, and the committee has approved it.

The process does not always move as smoothly as explained. The student may look at several topics and select one. He or she does some investigation but finds that the topic will not work out. The candidate selects another topic and develops a new proposal. The proposal, when first presented, has many uncertainties and ambiguities. By working with the committee, the proposal is finally made sharper and more definite until finally the exact task to be performed has been defined. The life cycle of a dissertation can thus be thought of as going from the general to the specific. The events that mark the reduction in generality until a dissertation is finally accepted are as follows:

1. Selection of general area for research
2. Selection of several topics for evaluation
3. Selection of one topic and completion of dissertation proposal

Work Months		Percentage
5	Writing, editing, and proofing	36%
5	Research and analysis	36%
1	Search prior research	7%
3	Topic search and proposal	21%
14		100%

2-4. Allocation of effort in a typical doctoral dissertation.

4. Completion of detailed chapter outlines
5. Completion of literature search
6. Completion of research
7. Completion of text of dissertation
8. Acceptance by committee

The systematic management plan described in the text will illustrate how to proceed through these general steps, how to use various methods to focus on the problem to be done, and how to obtain assistance from a dissertation committee and an advisor.

Figure 2-4 provides a general idea of how the time for a dissertation is spent. The time may vary considerably from these rough estimates. About one-third of the total hours will be occupied in writing the dissertation drafts, revising them, proofreading and correcting, and revising again. It comes as a surprise to many candidates that the actual writing occupies so much time. This will receive further explanation in Chapter 7.

The Overall Management Approach

The management approach described in this text has the following three major elements:
1. Predissertation stage activities
2. Selection of the dissertation topic
3. Management of research and writing

Each of these will be explained in detail in later chapters; the content of the three elements will be surveyed here. A checklist of major activities associated with the approach is found on the inside back cover.

PREDISSERTATION STAGE ACTIVITIES

If possible, the student should begin to think of the dissertation well before reaching dissertation stage. Ideally, the dissertation will initiate a line of research that can then be followed for some years. The choice should influence the planning of doctoral courses and especially the courses taken outside of the major field, such as research methodology and minor fields or supporting programs. The early selection of a research area will allow the candidate to obtain desirable background, do pre-dissertation investigation as part of coursework requirements, and develop committee contacts among professors who have an interest in the area. A student should begin, as soon as possible, to compile a dissertation topic file for cogent ideas, together with all the supporting evidence that is available at the time.

SELECTION OF THE DISSERTATION TOPIC

The selection of the dissertation topic is an iterative activity. Rarely does a student have a topic which is well defined in the beginning. Generally, the initial topic is poorly defined, too general, and too large in scope. It usually requires several iterations before the topic is refined and a good dissertation proposal is developed. The systematic management approach begins by examining several possibilities, putting these into a topic analysis format, consulting with the advisor and the committee, and selecting one of the topics to pursue in more detail. The selected topic is expanded into a dissertation proposal. The initial proposal is clarified, expanded, reduced, and refined, until it is sufficiently explicit so that the committee can agree it is an acceptable project of the scope and quality suitable for a doctoral dissertation.

MANAGEMENT OF RESEARCH AND WRITING

Every student working on a dissertation should draw up a schedule for completion. The plan should show the candidate how much time is available and provide a good idea of the amount of time that can be spent on each of the various activities required for the dissertation. The candidate should use various methods for improving the working relationship with the advisor and the committee. These include written documents, summaries of meetings and discussions, issue summaries and chapter outlines for chapters, and agendas for meetings. These activities generally help make the relationship of the advisor and the committee more productive. The candidate should actively plan and control the dissertation activities. A few hours each month spent in planning and control will generally increase the productivity of the work time.

CHAPTER 3

The Selection of an Advisor and a Dissertation Committee

The power and influence of the advisor is usually quite large in determining whether or not a candidate shall be allowed to continue in the doctoral program. Guidance from the advisor is usually a very significant factor, affecting the quality of the final dissertation. The selection of the advisor is therefore an important decision.

At some universities, advisors and committees are arbitrarily assigned. A candidate can usually work satisfactorily with most advisors and most committees. But in those cases where the candidate is able to influence the selection of the advisor and the committee, the student should seek to select the advisor and the committee that will provide the best assistance.

The Ideal Relationship

The ideal advisor for a candidate has characteristics such as the following:

1. The advisor is interested in the topic.
2. The advisor is competent to advise on the topic. This means that he or she must know enough to review the research and give sound advice.
3. The advisor has a reasonable level of expectations re-

garding what a student can and should accomplish in a doctoral dissertation.

4. The advisor reads and comments on dissertation documents within a reasonable time period.

5. The advisor is constant in his or her requirements and advice. He or she should not constantly add requirements and change advice already given.

6. The advisor has personal integrity. He or she views the advisor role as an important responsibility, deserving of a faculty member's attention.

7. The advisor is interested in the candidate as a person and is interested in the candidate's welfare, both as a person and as a scholar.

The advisor gives guidance and advice, acts as chairman of the committee, and is the one most able to protect the candidate from possible unfair demands by the dissertation committee. Therefore, a mutual respect is needed that allows the candidate to trust the advisor, and that allows the advisor to have confidence in the student. A candidate who does a good dissertation is a credit to the advisor. The advisor can take pride in the good work of his or her advisees. Therefore, an advisor favors a candidate who will do a good job.

The rest of the dissertation committee is important because they function in approving the dissertation. They can also be of great assistance in planning the dissertation and performing the research. The ideal committee will provide skills supportive to the candidate. A student doing an investigation involving human behavior may have one committee member interested and competent in the behavioral sciences and perhaps another who is competent to advise on the statistical analysis of the data. The criteria for a committee member are similar to those of an advisor, but the committee member should, if possible, complement the advisor. The advisor must work with the committee and must feel comfortable with them. If the option is allowed, the student should suggest a committee, but he or she should be prepared to suggest alternative members in order to provide some flexibility for the advisor in proposing a committee.

The committee, and especially the advisor, are likely to be important in facilitating a candidate's career. Normally, the best assistance in obtaining an academic position comes from an advisor and the rest of the committee. Joint research and publishing with the advisor or others on the committee are factors that may establish a significant professional relationship and continuing friendship.

The personal relationship between faculty and the doctoral candidate should be that of senior and junior colleague. The dissertation marks the last major step toward independent professional status. However, the dissertation is the candidate's, not the advisor's or the committee's, dissertation.

Analyzing Alternative Advisors and Committee Members

If an advisor and a committee are assigned to a candidate, then an analysis is unnecessary. But in most cases, the candidate has considerable latitude in proposing a committee. There is no way to be completely certain that the best advisor has been chosen. However, some factors, such as the following, can provide evidence for the decision process.

1. *Past performance with other candidates* In a large department of twenty professors authorized to be advisors, the doctoral candidates will tend to cluster around four or five professors who have shown an interest and an ability in assisting candidates. Some faculty members have never advised a candidate who finished a dissertation. In considering potential advisors, a recent past

record of successful candidates is an important plus factor. The recency of the record may be important, since some professors change in their orientation to students. The criteria should be approached cautiously, however, because some professors have not had the opportunity to have doctoral advisees, so these criteria are not applicable to them.

2. *Interest and competence in topic area or research methodology* The interest of a prospective advisor does not have to be specific to the candidate's topic, but it should include the general area or the research methodology being used. Competence is the ability to understand a candidate's plan and project, in order to provide sound advice.

3. *Personality and personal characteristics* Are the personalities of the candidate and the advisor compatible? Does the advisor demonstrate integrity in criticism? Does the advisor demonstrate personal integrity in dealings with students and advisees? Discussion with a faculty member's current candidates can often be helpful in assessing the "style" of the advisor, the manner of providing support, his or her capacity to offer critical assistance, and availability.

4. *Response characteristics* An advisor may be very good, but may procrastinate reading and commenting on student materials. This may be due to personal habits, or it may be due to an excessive overall workload.

It is impossible to quantify the process of selecting an advisor. It is impossible to quantify the factors that are important in selecting an advisor. Each candidate should review the factors and decide their importance in his or her situation, keeping in mind the goal of timely completion.

The committee members may also be evaluated in much the same way. The competence and interest characteristics of potential committee members are very significant. Two major criteria for selection are the assistance a proposed committee member is likely to provide to the candidate and the advisor's feeling as to how the proposed committee member will function in the committee.

The Ideal Candidate

The previous discussion described the ideal advisor. The ideal candidate, from the standpoint of the advisor and the committee, is one with whom they feel they can be effective. They generally want a candidate—

1. who will do a good dissertation they can be proud to sign, and who will do it in a reasonable time;
2. who shows initiative, but accepts guidance and follows through on suggestions;
3. who is organized and uses the committee's time effectively, and who is also reasonable in the demands on their time;
4. with personal integrity.

A candidate shows these characteristics by the way he or she interacts with the advisor and the committee. If predissertation activities have provided good interaction with the faculty members (described in the next chapter), a good relationship may already have been established. In other cases, the candidate gives indicators of future performance by the way he or she approaches the dissertation project.

Professors will be much more willing to serve on a committee if the candidate demonstrates that the time demands will be reasonable, that their time will be used effectively, and that a good dissertation will result. A student who follows the systematic management approach is likely to demonstrate that he or she meets these criteria.

CHAPTER **4**

Predissertation Development Activities

Students frequently wait until they have completed all requirements except the dissertation before seriously considering the dissertation topic. The difficulty with this approach is that there are many dissertation topics which they cannot then handle because they have not had the proper background in terms of course work or other study. This chapter proposes a plan in which the student selects the general area of the dissertation while course work is being planned. The candidate then uses the courses to do predissertation development. This insures that the necessary course work and statistical and mathematical tools needed for the dissertation project will be available. The benefits from early selection of a topic are also applicable to a master's thesis.

Not all students are able to do the predissertation development activities proposed in the chapter. Some students do not make a commitment to the doctorate until their course work has begun. Other students have difficulty in deciding even on a general area for scholarly inquiry. Then, some students find it difficult to think about a dissertation when they are concentrating on completing the course work, passing the qualifying examinations, and meeting other requirements. However, students who cannot do all of the predissertation development activities should, as a minimum, establish dissertation topic files very early in their doctoral work.

Selection of General Area for Investigation

The basis for the predissertation development activities is early selection of the topic area for the dissertation. Topic area in this case is usually very large and very general. For example, a student in management might select planning as a general area for investigation. Or the topic may be narrowed to strategic planning. No attempt is made at this time to narrow the general area into a thesis topic. With a tentative selection of a general area for investigation, the student should take the earliest opportunity to do some investigation and reading in the area, giving special attention to the type of research skills that were necessary for the research being reviewed, as well as the general background that would be useful for someone doing research in the area.

EXAMPLE 1: In the case of planning, the student might find that some research has used survey and interviewing techniques to obtain data about current practices in government and industry, while other investigations have used computer simulation. The investigations have generally required an understanding of the psychological nature of humans in a planning situation. This knowledge can be useful in planning course work in psychology.

EXAMPLE 2: A student interested in the outcomes of counseling and psychotherapy might discover that assessment has been done using field research (actual therapy cases), analogue studies (simulated laboratory counseling), and basic psychological laboratory research. He or she might find that there was a need to show correspondence between particular counseling strategies and particular outcomes, as well as to link counselor personality traits and client problems. Such awareness can be useful in the selection of course work including the needed methodological statistical design courses.

Course Work in Predissertation Development

Most students, when planning their course work for the doctorate, have a number of required courses. However, there generally are a number of courses which are optional for the student. The choice of a minor, or supporting, program is generally left to the student. Rather than haphazardly selecting a minor, the student should consider the areas that will be needed as support for a future dissertation project. For instance, a student who is interested in planning and who already has reasonable skills in quantitative techniques, such as simulation, might decide to emphasize certain survey techniques for data collection in the research methodology course. He or she should take a minor in psychology, sociology, or some set of courses which support an understanding of human behavior in organizations.

The student can use the courses to help solidify ideas and get suggestions for ways to approach the dissertation topics. For example, as the student proceeds with course work, he or she may perceive that there will be a need to collect data from organizations. While taking a course in survey methodology, the candidate might use course problems to help in formulating a survey plan for possible use in the dissertation research. If the course requires a project, the student might develop a test of a possible data collection plan for the class project. The student might take a course in psychology which discusses experiments showing risk aversion tendencies in humans and the relationship to human behavior in planning situations. A paper or other project in the course might provide an opportunity for the student to explore the relevance of this research to the general area of dissertation interest.

The use of course work in predissertation development has another advantage. The student is able to come in contact with potential committee members. The student becomes acquainted with professors in classroom situations and learns their interests. In connection with papers and other projects required for class, the student is able to discuss the dissertation area. The course instructors might make very useful suggestions on how the student could structure a research project in the area.

Dissertation Ideas File

Dissertation ideas occur at strange times—while shaving, at the movies, working on an unrelated course problem. The wise student will immediately write down and file each idea that seems remotely worthwhile. While reading journal articles or listening to talks, ideas are often presented that might make feasible dissertations. Alternative research plans often come to mind when reading research results. If the topic is a result of a suggestion made in a journal article, this should be carefully referenced so that the reference will not have to be searched a second time. All of these ideas should be kept in a dissertation idea file. The file may consist of a notebook or a set of file folders, but each idea should be written down immediately. Every six months or so, each idea can be organized into a skeleton outline, known as the topic analysis form (to be presented in Chapter 6). This outline form indicates the general topic or the hypothesis, why it might be important, the general methodology, the possible outcomes, and the contribution to knowledge. The purpose of putting the ideas in this form is to start thinking about dissertation topics in an organized way. However, the main thing is to build up a file of interesting topics. Investigation and selection can be done later.

Risks and Alternatives

There appear to be substantial advantages in thinking ahead to the dissertation. If it is possible to select a general area for investigation, then course work should be supportive of that topic. Work within the courses should be used as much as possible. The student should become acquainted with faculty members who have interests that would support the dissertation. If the dissertation develops as anticipated, predissertation development activities are likely to be very valuable, reduce the total time for the dissertation, and allow improvement in the quality of the dissertation. However, there is some risk in this strategy. The general area selected early in doctoral work may not become the area of the dissertation. The candidate may arrange a program around one general area and find that it does not support the final topic. To balance the benefits and the risks, students should generally take a good, solid set of courses related to doctoral research, but include some courses which support the general area tentatively chosen. The assigned papers and projects in course work should still be used as opportunities to investigate potential dissertation topics or to do preliminary work.

5

The Selection of a Dissertation Topic

Most students have a difficult time visualizing a doctoral dissertation (or master's thesis). The discussion of contribution to knowledge and scope of topics seems very abstract at first. The standard of quality is so vague as to be meaningless. The student is likely to get responses such as the following:

Question	*Typical Answer*
What are the quality standards?	High!
How long does a dissertation have to be?	Long enough to develop the subject properly!
How exhaustive should the literature survey be?	Fairly exhaustive!

Rather than trying to define quality, length, style, and other requirements, the student should examine a set of dissertations (or master's theses). Dissertations (and some master's theses) for each university are generally filed in the library; dissertations accepted by other universities may be obtained (1) from other university libraries via interlibrary loan, or (2) from University Microfilms, Ann Arbor, Michigan (for American and some European dissertations); abstracts of dissertations are published in *Dissertation Abstracts International,* a reference generally available in a research library. Master's theses from other universities may usually be obtained through interlibrary loan if the awarding university requires a copy to be placed in the library (which many do not require).

Some suggestions for dissertations a student might examine are as follows:

1. Award-winning dissertations in the candidate's field or related fields (such as the Ford Foundation awards for dissertations in Business and dissertation award of The Society for the Psychological Study of Social Issues)
2. Recent dissertations in the selected field at various universities
3. Good recent dissertations as suggested by faculty in the department
4. The best dissertations suggested by the advisor

In reading dissertations, the student should begin to formulate a general understanding of the structure and scope of a dissertation, and the meaning of contribution to knowledge as applied to doctoral dissertations. Discussions with other students, faculty, and the advisor are also helpful.[1]

Characteristics of a Good Dissertation Topic

No dissertation topic is perfect. However, in searching for a topic, certain characteristics should be kept in mind as being important.

1. Need for research
2. Amenable to research methods
3. Achievable in reasonable time
4. Symmetry of potential outcomes
5. Matches student capabilities and interest
6. Attractive for funding
7. Area for professional development

The dissertation must make a contribution to knowledge, but

---

[1]*See also* M. M. Chambers: "Selection, Definition and Delimitation of a Doctoral Research Problem," *Phi Delta Kappan,* 42 (3), (1963): 71-73.

this important element will be discussed in a separate section of the chapter.

NEED FOR RESEARCH

There should be a need for the research, and it should be significant or important; otherwise, the research should not be conducted. This does not mean that the results must have immediate application, but rather that the topic should not be trivial or of little importance. The student should also feel the problem is important and worthwhile because there will be periods of routine work, and enthusiasm for the project helps to keep it moving during such times. The need to understand the nature of things is the motivation for much research that has no immediate use, but there should be some need, importance, or significance in knowing the result. For example, a student might think about research on the color preferences of school principals. It is very possible to get such data and analyze it, but the results are probably not important.

AMENABLE TO RESEARCH METHODS

The topic needs to be feasible regarding both availability of data and availability of tools for analysis. There are many interesting problems that cannot be researched because no suitable research methods exist, or data cannot be obtained. Some research methods may be unacceptable because of government or university regulations. For example, the U. S. Department of Health, Education and Welfare requires universities to establish and police guidelines for research involving human subjects. It should also be noted that some research methods are beyond the capabilities of students because of technical, cost, or time requirements. A topic which is probably not amenable to doctoral research is a proposal to study the causes of the United States' failure to win the Vietnam war. The number of factors which impinged on that particular set of events was very large and included the decisions made by several presidents over a twenty-year period. The interrelatedness of these complex events would be indeterminable during the period of time, and with the resources normally available to a Ph.D. candidate.

ACHIEVABLE IN REASONABLE TIME

The normal amount of required time for a doctoral thesis probably varies from university to university. However, rather than leaving "reasonable time" completely undefined, some rough estimates will be presented which the student must translate to the situation of his or her university.

The range of time for most dissertations is probably from twelve to seventeen work months, the elapsed time usually being longer because of part-time work and similar delays. The background investigation, definition of problem, and writing normally take more than half of the total time. This rough computation suggests that the running of experiments, data collection, data analysis, theory formulation, and other activities, should be achievable in from four to eight work months (probably close to six). Since many activities occur in parallel (e.g., writing of chapter on prior research while collecting data), the time span over which data collection, analysis, and other activities, can occur may be from eight to twelve months. A student may wish to select a topic having a longer time requirement, but should do so with an awareness of the consequences for the date of completion. An illustration of a topic which does not meet the completion time criterion is a dissertation topic which proposes to study the development of college students from the freshman to senior years. This is a study which would have to extend over four or more years and, therefore, normally would not be suitable as a dissertation topic. Time limitations may sometimes be overcome by alternative research designs. In the above example, the topic may be studied in a shorter time by taking measurements for two groups that are matched by characteristics, one group consisting of freshman students, the other group composed of senior students. However, such cross-sectioned studies have severe limitations, resulting from potentially different subject characteristics which develop over time, dropouts from college, and different selection criteria.

SYMMETRY OF POTENTIAL OUTCOMES

A research project will typically have more than one potential outcome. For example, a research experiment may fail to disprove the hypothesis, it may disprove it, or it may be inconclusive. An algorithm for solving a class of problems will either work or not work.

The ideal dissertation topic is one in which (given a careful methodology) any of the potential outcomes would be satisfactory in terms of dissertation acceptability. For example, a student may have a hypothesis that two alternative teaching methodologies will have differential outcomes. If the experiment is well conducted, and if the research design and statistical procedures are appropriate, then confirming the hypothesis is an important result, with implications for teaching a particular subject matter. However, the opposite is also interesting. If it is shown that neither teaching method has a clear advantage over the other, this is just as important a conclusion, because either method can be used, depending on considerations other than outcomes.

As an example of nonsymmetrical outcomes, a hypothesis which says that one can predict decision-making style from characteristics of an executive turns out to be important in only one case. If this hypothesis is confirmed, and the prediction can be made with reasonable accuracy, the result is interesting. But suppose there is to be no correlation. This is not nearly as interesting, and it probably would not be a significant contribution.

This lack of symmetry applies to most dissertations involving new algorithms or solutions procedures. If the algorithm is found, there is a good dissertation. If no algorithm is found, a contribution has not been made. Note, however, that if a solution method has been proposed by one or more authorities but not proved, then a dissertation might proceed to prove or disprove the fact that this algorithm can be used. Then, proving that the algorithm is feasible, or showing that it does not work in a particular situation (since it was thought to be feasible) are both contributions to knowledge.

MATCH WITH STUDENT CAPABILITIES AND INTEREST

A topic should match the capabilities and interest of the student. A student who has strong capabilities in the behavioral sciences and low mathematical capabilities should certainly not choose a mathematical dissertation involving proofs and algorithms, even though it might be otherwise a good topic. Likewise, a student with strong mathematical capabilities and very little interest or training in behavioral science should not choose a topic which depends for its success upon high ability and training in that field.

ATTRACTIVE FOR FUNDING

In a pure scholarly sense, funding should not really be a consideration. But most students who are doing dissertation research have a sufficiently broad range of possibilities that they can choose among alternatives. When selecting among alternatives, a student might consider the likelihood that each topic will attract the necessary funding. Topics which are current and have some unusual approach are usually most likely to obtain funding.

AREA FOR PROFESSIONAL DEVELOPMENT

A dissertation may either be a beginning of research on a topic or it may be the end. A student puts a significant amount of work into a dissertation topic and, therefore, becomes one of the most knowledgeable scholars on that subject. If there is likely to be a continuing interest, either academically or elsewhere in the topic, then he or she can continue to maintin scholarly capability in the area and continue to be a significant authority on the subject. A student can, therefore, make the dissertation a career stepping stone by selecting a topic that provides development in areas in which he or she is likely to work. Since there is a great deal of risk in the dissertation research, a student will usually select a topic in an area which is characterized by some prior research, rather than a completely new area for research. "Exploratory" research is usually too underdefined to allow a student to demonstrate competency, and it often results in asymmetrical results. On the other hand, candidates need to avoid overworked areas where they would be merely reworking someone else's ideas and not making a contribution of their own.

Sources of Potential Topics

A student generally has some idea of one or more general areas in which to search for a topic. There are several fruitful sources for identifying potential dissertation topics.

1. *Current events* The current events or popular journals often describe problems relating to social welfare, business, economics, education, and government before the scholarly journals in a field recognize them as problems requiring research. One reason for this is the delay in publication by many scholarly journals (a one-year delay after acceptance is not unusual). For example, it was

clear from the news media that pornography would be a social issue well before the presidential commission on pornography was appointed. A doctoral student in sociology, in the early 1960s, would have been able to identify the emerging problem from the news media (and perhaps from scholarly journals as well).

2. *Suggestions for research from past dissertations*   As soon as a student has an interest in an area, he or she should obtain copies of dissertations that have been written in the area. The method of search is presented later in this chapter. Writers of dissertations frequently describe further research which needs to be done. The suggestions are potentially valuable since they come from persons who have done research in the area.

3. *Suggestions for research by authorities in the field*   Generally, there are a few well-known authorities in a field, and in articles or speeches, they often comment on the need for research. Frequently an article or a committee report will be issued specifically on the need for research in an area.

4. *Expressions of need for research by practitioners in a field*   In the field of management, a well-known and well-regarded manager may describe the areas where he or she feels there is insufficient evidence on which to base decision making. These suggestions must be viewed cautiously, since the practitioners are frequently not aware of research that has been done. However, this provides a good starting point for further investigation.

5. *Generally accepted but unproved suppositions*   Every field of knowledge or endeavor has a large number of suppositions or accepted ideas that no one has ever bothered to test or validate. For example, one highly regarded and widely used text in reading and study skills proposed a system for studying that was quoted for twenty

years but never systematically tested. Subsequent tests of the method failed to find any evidence for its assertions. Indeed, evidence was found for a much simpler technique that could be taught more easily with more effective results.

6. *Unproved or weakly proved assertions by an authority in the field* Authorities in the field frequently will make unproved or poorly proved assertations. These need to be tested and subjected to further analysis. For example, a well-known researcher may assert that capital budgeting techniques are used as a control mechanism rather than as the basis for decision making. He may say that he has never seen a company that actually used them for decision-making purposes. Therefore, he reasons, the extreme emphasis on capital budgeting techniques and upon the refining of the techniques is misplaced. This assertion by an authority in the field can obviously be proved or disproved by accumulating evidence from research.

7. *Different approaches to testing of important results* If a researcher has reported interesting research results with one research technique and a given research population, a doctoral student may consider replicating the experiment. but altering either the research technique or the research population. One researcher might study consumer reaction to price changes by bringing housewives into a laboratory setting where they were asked to rate the importance of price differences on the purchase decision. Another researcher might replicate the essence of the experiment but use after-purchase interviews with housewives who have just made a purchase, thereby changing the experimental technique. In another experiment, one researcher might conduct a simulation using college students to find that attitude change is highly correlated with the physical attractiveness of the influencer. Such a simu-

lation conducted with college students can be replicated using housewives' attitudes toward particular market products, or with working men's attitudes toward political issues. In fact, when significant results are obtained in the college laboratory using students, it is useful to replicate the experiment in the real environment or population to determine if the results still hold. There is some evidence to suggest that the artificiality of students as subjects may induce incorrect results.

The Contribution of a Dissertation

A requirement for almost all doctoral dissertations is that they make a contribution to knowledge. It is difficult to define precisely the meaning of the term "contribution to knowledge." What is acceptable at one university might not be acceptable at another. One advisor might accept what another may reject. The dissertation should be based on a significant question, problem, or hypothesis. The work should be original and should relate to, explain, solve, or add proof to the question, problem or hypothesis. The research adds to knowledge and usually results in the formation of generalizations. The additive contributrion of a dissertation may arise from—

1. new or improved evidence;
2. new or improved methodology;
3. new or improved analysis.

The contribution of a dissertation may be based on more than one of these. For example, a dissertation might develop some theory, obtain empirical data, and integrate the two.

NEW OR IMPROVED EVIDENCE

The evidence in a dissertation may disprove or support a concept, theory, or model. Evidence may disprove or support a hypothesis, or it may add to the understanding of a process. Major questions regarding evidence are:

How were the data collected?

How were the data analyzed?

The evidence may be collected by an experiment, simulation, questionnaire, interviews, or measurements. A major question regarding such evidence is the method by which it was obtained. If a researcher asks, "Are you prejudiced?," and if 95% of the respondents say "no," does this provide solid evidence? Almost certainly not because most people, prejudiced or not, will tend to answer "no." The technique is faulty, so the results are faulty.

The method of analysis is likewise very significant. Reporting the means of badly skewed distributions is misleading; not providing the changes in the variance of a distribution may lead to wrong conclusions. For example, in the field of psychotherapy outcome, research was reported for years in terms of mean changes. When one researcher began to examine changes in variance he discovered that a proportion of patients got worse and a proportion got better. Results that had looked like "no change" now had to be examined for "deterioration" effects as well as gains.

NEW OR IMPROVED METHODOLOGY

The contribution can be a new or improved solution or analysis procedure (such as a new statistical procedure) or a new or improved research methodology (such as a new method for obtaining data on personality disorders). Showing the benefit of applying a known procedure in a new way may also be a contribution.

Improvement from a new or changed methodology or solution procedure should be significant. For example, a dissertation showing that a new solution algorithm for correlation coefficients can reduce errors in the result at the fourth decimal place is not worthy of acceptance as a doctoral dissertation. Correlation coefficients are rarely significant beyond two places, if that. However, if the new solution procedure should be applied to significant computational problems, it might be a contribution.

Quantitative solution procedures can be demonstrated by proofs and examples. Other solution procedures may need to be supplemented by evidence of their efficacy. For example, a student may propose (and support with conceptual reasoning) a new solution procedure for developing a strategic plan for an organization (such as a business). Unless there is supporting evidence, the mere assertion that this is a successful solution procedure is probably not sufficient. A single-case example may often be sufficient to demonstrate its feasibility. In such an instance, testing its relative efficacy compared to other methods is probably another dissertation topic and may be left for another researcher.

NEW OR IMPROVED ANALYSIS

Analysis may be based on existing evidence or include new data. The following are some examples of types of analysis.

1. *Historical analysis*   Ideas or historical forces are developed. An example is an economic interpretation of the American Revolution.

2. *Analysis of implications of a current development in a field*   An example is an analysis of the impact of transaction analysis on counseling.

3. *Comparative analysis*   Theories, methodologies, or systems are compared. An example is a comparison of management theory in capitalist and socialist environments.

4. *Analysis of an existing theory or concept and its implications*   An example is an analysis of the theory of cognitive dissonance.

The method of analysis may be important. There are usually generally accepted methods in a field. For example, there are methods for historical analysis and for analysis of economic theories, as well as methods for experimental analysis. In other cases there are no generally accepted approaches. The student may need to innovate, but he or she may find it useful to first consider applying known techniques, accepted as valid in other fields, before embarking on untried methods of analysis.

NEW OR IMPROVED CONCEPTS OR THEORIES

Concepts, theories, or models are developed to explain phenomena in a field or to provide structure or framework to knowledge in a field. An entirely new concept, theory, or model may be developed, or an existing concept, theory, or model may be enlarged or extended. In such a concept or theory dissertation, it is usually desirable to illustrate how the theory, concept, or model can be used to explain, predict, or understand.

Projects Not Generally Accepted as a Dissertation

It is generally agreed that literature surveys or descriptive compilations do not meet the contribution-to-knowledge requirement for the dissertation. State-of-the-art descriptions, no matter how well done, are generally not accepted. For example, a good textbook may be excellent in terms of contribution to teaching, but it is not generally considered to fulfill the contribution-to-knowledge requirement because textbooks tend to report the existing state of the art. A literature survey is included as part of most dissertations but this cannot be the main contribution of a dissertation.

An historical survey is not usually considered to be a contribution to knowledge unless accompanied by some analysis or testing of the historical ideas. For example, an historical survey of the development of some industry, such as the steel industry in the United States, might not be considered a satisfactory dissertation. However, if there is some underlying concept or analysis of the reason why the steel industry developed as it did, then this research would probably be accepted as a dissertation. A description of American commerce during the American Revolution might be somewhat weak as a dissertation, but a description of American commerce as it relates to an economic interpretation of history might be considered to be a good dissertation.

There is some disagreement about the contribution made from single-case descriptions. In general, however, a case description of a single situation is probably not a satisfactory dissertation unless it is used as an illustration of an underlying structure, theory, or concept. In other words, a theory might be proposed, and then a single-case description might be used to illustrate the underlying theory.

Development projects which apply known knowledge are usually not thought to fulfill the requirements for dissertations (unless there are some comparative results). Developing and installing a performance evaluation system in an organization such as a business, university, or government agency may be a very creative activity, but it is probably not a dissertation. A student might write a set of computer programs to do statistical analysis. This may be a very worthwhile project, but it does not represent a doctoral dissertation—not because it lacks substantial work, or even importance, to the users, but because it represents a development project which does not add to knowledge. On the other hand, a dissertation project which proposes a behavioral theory to explain the use and nonuse of statistical packages, collects data showing the reasons packages are not used, develops a software package which overcomes these deficiencies, applies this software in an experimental setting, and then obtains statistics which show that the new approach does actually produce better results would probably be considered an acceptable dissertation. Note the differences, however. The software package in the second dissertation was merely a means of collecting data to prove an underlying concept.

Investigating Existing Knowledge on a Topic

An important part of the search for a topic is an investigation of existing knowledge and current research in the topic area. The investigation proceeds conceptually through the following three stages with increasing scope and depth.

1. Exploratory investigations, as part of the development and evaluation of possible topics in an area
2. Investigation in some depth, sufficient to support a formal research and dissertation proposal
3. Complete research that is described in the "literature/research" section of the dissertation

The literature/current research is a significant part not only of the topic selection, but also of the entire dissertation process. Because of the vast store of knowledge and the increasing rate at which knowledge is being accumulated, it is important that the researcher become efficient in the search. A full treatise of this subject is beyond the scope of this book. However, we are able to suggest a framework for initiating the search and a search strategy. Appendix I contains a list of frequently used tools and techniques for bibliographic search.

FRAMEWORK FOR INITIATING THE SEARCH

Admundson[2] has suggested that a searcher consider both the *bibliographic chain* and the means of *bibliographic control.* A

---

[2] Colleen Admundson, Unpublished paper, 1973.

bibliographic chain refers to the channels through which an idea moves, as it progresses from a new idea to a formal study and eventually is incorporated into conventional knowledge. For example, a researcher may discover a new idea about a certain phenomenon while analyzing data on a project. The idea might be discussed with colleagues and students but not be known outside that close circle. Then the institution may allocate local "seed" money for investigation. If productive, external funding may be sought, and the idea captured in a grant proposal. When the formal research is completed, technical reports are prepared. Only when the idea is well formulated and initial confirmatory data are available is the idea published—often years after the work is completed. These published reports most frequently are found in professional periodicals. When extensive research has been done the report may appear in a monograph of some length. The more extensive research is often abstracted and collated with other related work and included in books. As those books are used, the idea becomes part of the body of knowledge in the field. The bibliographic chain explains why current research is difficult to locate—it is either not published, or it appears in obscure technical reports and hard-to-find periodicals.

Bibliographic control refers to the various means by which a researcher locates the published and unpublished material related to an area of investigation. Figure 5-1 shows how bibliographic control interfaces with the bibliographic chain. The missing elements in Figure 5-1 are ways of locating early work in progress. These methods are mostly informal ways of engaging in a network of researchers. Seminars and colloquia are ways of finding out the most recent thinking of researchers in the field. Conferences and conventions provide opportunities for work in progress to be reported. Entering into the network is most effectively done by personal contacts with

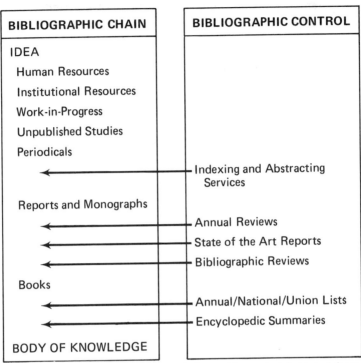

5-1. A bibliographic chain with bibliographic control (adapted from Admundson, Unpublished paper, 1973.)

other researchers. These contacts can sometimes be made at conferences and conventions. Contacts are often made through personal letters. Such personal contacts are often difficult for doctoral students to make, but they can be developed with some assistance from an advisor and some initiative on the part of the student.

It should be obvious that the newer the ideas are, the more difficult they are to obtain. The more general and well known information is easier to locate. Thus, finding the information needed to refine a research topic into a researchable idea, with the potential for contributing to the body of knowledge, will usually take considerable time and the candidate should allow for it.

ELEMENTS IN A SEARCH STRATEGY

A search of the literature related to a potential topic should not be a haphazard, random process. A search at any of the three levels (exploratory, proposal, and dissertation chapter) will be most effective if the researcher plans a search strategy that is most likely to provide the depth and scope needed for a given stage of the dissertation. All search strategies assume that the researcher has become familiar with basic library guides to reference materials. A representative list is contained in Appendix I. The appendix also describes the computer-search tools for searching literature. Reference librarians should be consulted at appropriate points in a search.

It is important to a successful search strategy to identify useful descriptors or search terms. Start a list of terms you consider relevant. Check to see if these terms are used as library subject headings by looking up the terms in the United States Library of Congress, *Library of Congress Subject Heading,* or Minnie Earle Sears' *List of Subject Headings,* 10th ed. (New York: Wilson, 1972). Although the terms listed in these references will not necessarily be the subject headings used in the periodical indexes or data bases, they will help in the location of books in the library card catalog. Another source of useful subject headings are the tracings at the bottom of every catalog card.

The following elements can be combined into an appropriate search strategy.

1. Search for dissertations, using manual search of the *Comprehensive Dissertation Index* or computer search, using DATRIX dissertation search service. Examine abstracts of dissertations in *Dissertation Abstracts International.*

Obtain copies of selected dissertations from Xerox University Microfilms or through interlibrary loan. Use bibliographies in dissertations for literature leads.

2. Examine books related to the subject. Check their bibliographies and references. Find the section of the library stacks with books on the subject and make a quick search of all the books. However, some books may be checked out, so examine the "shelf list" (a set of cards in shelf order) for the library.

3. Search indexing services for journal literature. Typical examples of indexes are as follows:
   - *Index to Legal Periodicals*
   - *Business Periodicals Index*
   - *Applied Science and Technology Index*
   - *Public Affairs Information Service*
   - *New York Times Index*

4. Search indexes in the abstracting service available in your field. Use printed index and/or computer search of index or abstract. Typical examples of abstracting services are as follows:
   - *Psychological Abstracts*
   - *Chemical Abstracts*
   - *Biological Abstracts*

5. Search government publications using sources such as the *Monthly Catalog of U.S. Government Publications* or NTIS search, as described in Appendix I.

6. Search bibliographies in journal articles and research reports. Check for specialized bibliographies by societies and associations.

7. Search annual indexes in scholarly journals not otherwise searched.

INVESTIGATING PRIOR DOCTORAL RESEARCH

Students doing dissertation topic search are usually familiar with standard journal search processes but overlook the prior-dissertation search. Recent doctoral dissertations are important in the search because the information is relatively current (not subject to publication lag), usually presented in detail (often lacking in periodicals), and often includes an extensive bibliography which can lead to additional resources.

Because of the special importance of a search of prior dissertations on the topic or on closely related topics, the major sources of dissertations will be explained (and summarized in Appendix I). American doctoral dissertations are listed in three major sources:

1. *American Doctoral Dissertations;* previously published as *Index to American Doctoral Dissertations* and *Doctoral Dissertations Accepted by American Universities* Published under the auspices of the Association of Research Libraries, dissertation titles are listed under broad academic disciplines such as Biology, and Agriculture. There is a fourteen-twenty month delay in the listing of a new dissertation. A student should search the listing for titles that appear interesting. A copy can be obtained through interlibrary loan. The request is made to the student's library, which requests the loan. Or the student may write to the researcher if a current address can be found. (One possibility for finding addresses is professional association directories to which the researcher is likely to belong.) The advantages of *American Doctoral Dissertations* is that it is very complete; the disadvantages are the listing of only the title and no finer breakdowns to facilitate search, and the difficulties sometimes encountered in locating a copy of the dissertation.

2. *Comprehensive Dissertation Index 1861-1972 with annual supplements for subsequent years* This is the most comprehensive list of doctoral dissertations, listing virtually every doctoral dissertation awarded since American doc-

toral programs began. It includes all listings found in *American Doctoral Dissertations.* There is a five-volume author index and thirty-two volumes, divided by discipline. There is a cross reference if the dissertation is abstracted in *Dissertation Abstracts International.* A key word-in-title index is used.

3. *Dissertation Abstracts International* This is a listing of U. S. doctoral dissertations together with an abstract of each dissertation. There is a three- to twelve-month delay in listing a new dissertation. Starting with 1966, many Canadian universities are also listed, and from 1975, many European dissertations are included. A complete microfilm copy, or a hard copy from the microfilm, is available from the publisher: Xerox/University Microfilms, Ann Arbor, Michigan. Extending back to 1938, under the name of *Dissertation Abstracts* or *Microfilm Abstracts,* the journal is published monthly. The listings are divided into broad categories. There are two series, starting with June 1966—A, for Social Science and B, for Physical Science. To search all issues can be quite time consuming. Two methods are used to reduce search time:

   a. *Key word-in-title index.* Beginning with July 1969 (Volume XXX), there is a key word index in each issue, plus an author index. At the end of the July to June year, the monthly indices for the year are published as a cumulative index. Prior to 1969, an index was published as *Dissertation Abstracts International Retrospective Index.* The same type of key word index is used in the *Comprehensive Dissertation Index 1861-1972.* The key word index lists the dissertation under every key word in the title (eliminating *the, and, large,* etc.). For example, all dissertations having the key word "budget" anywhere in the title are listed together. A dissertation titled "An

Inquiry into a Theory of Learning" would be listed under "inquiry," "theory," and "learning."

b. *DATRIX*. Operated by Xerox/University Microfilms, DATRIX (the latest revision is termed DATRIX II) is a computer-based retrieval system for locating dissertations using key words in the title. Instructions for use are obtained by writing to DATRIX, Xerox/University Microfilms, Ann Arbor, Michigan. The student specifies a set of search terms. The computer searches a file of dissertation titles and lists all titles containing the terms, plus the reference to *Dissertation Abstracts International* or other sources where the abstract may be found. The search is not perfect because a dissertation on the subject may not, for various reasons, use any of the terms in the title. On balance, however, it is a valuable and fairly inexpensive (approximately $15-$25) search procedure to use in the early stages of investigation.

The problem with *Dissertation Abstracts International* is the fact that it is not complete. Over 300 universities list dissertations, but many make listing voluntary; so some candidates never get around to sending in the dissertation. Also, there are a small number of major American universities which do not (for some strange reason) provide dissertations for microfilming and listing in *Dissertation Abstracts International*. These holdouts are slowly joining, so check the latest listing of participants. The student must obtain dissertations from the nonparticipating schools through interlibrary loan. On the other hand, the percentage of coverage is quite good. One estimate[3] is close to 80 percent of recent U. S. dissertations (since approximately 1964) are listed in *Dissertation Abstracts International* and the percentage of listings is increasing (probably over 95 percent by 1978.)

---

[3]Julie L. Moore, "Bibliographic Control of American Doctoral Dissertations," *Special Libraries,* (July 1972): 287.

CHAPTER 6

The Dissertation Proposal

The part of the dissertation project with which students seem to have the most difficulty is the preparation of a dissertation proposal outlining the research. It is a difficult activity, but one that is crucial in order to achieve the objective of timely completion. The proposal represents the blueprints for the dissertation. If the blueprints are clear and well done, the work can proceed with assurance; if incomplete and unclear, there is likely to be considerable misdirected effort.

The process of preparing a dissertation proposal is iterative. The student prepares a proposal and solicits reactions from advisor, committee, and colleagues. Based on these comments, the candidate prepares a revision. This is criticized and a new revision is prepared. There may be an opportunity for the candidate to present the proposal to a seminar. The comments will result in further revision. The process should continue until the proposal is a clear, crisp definition of the research project. This approach to development of a dissertation proposal is equally effective in preparing a master's thesis proposal.

The use of topic analysis forms to outline topics is recommended in the formative stages when several alternative topics are being considered. When one topic is chosen, the topic analysis can be expanded into a dissertation proposal. The dissertation proposal then proceeds through several iterations until the research is sufficiently well defined for the proposal to be accepted.

The Topic Analysis

A student will usually consider several possible dissertation topics, or alterntive approaches to the same problem, prior to selecting a final topic. The various possible topics should be analyzed as early as possible in terms of their suitability. A student who talks vaguely about doing a thesis on decision making in organizations does not yet have a dissertation topic because, within that general area, one might construct hundreds of possible dissertations. The problem is to identify several topics, prepare a topic analysis for each, and then choose the one which best meets the selection criteria. Unless the advisor has a specific problem in mind for the student to undertake, the student will get better advice by presenting several alternative analyses to the advisor or committee than by bringing in only one. The alternatives also act as a catalyst for bringing out fresh ideas as the student discusses the area of proposed investigation.

THE TOPIC ANALYSIS FORM

The topic analysis is essentially a simplified proposal form, providing a rough outline of factors relating to a dissertation. The parts are as follows:

1. Problem, hypothesis, or question
2. Importance of research (why it is worthy of doctoral research)
3. Significant prior research
4. Possible research approach or methodology
5. Potential outcomes of research and importance of each

Figure 6-1 is an example of a topic analysis. The topic analysis should be quite short—two to four pages should be sufficient in most cases. A short, concise description is needed at this juncture. A few comments about each section may help in preparing this type of analysis.

TOPIC ANALYSIS

*Student*____Clark G. Flint_____*Date*____September 29, 19—

1. Problem, Hypothesis, or Question

> Decision models are built to handle risk aversion by the users, but human decision makers are erratic in risk aversion responses.
>
> Major questions in area are:
>   1. What are the major determinants of variations in risk aversion behavior by human decision makers?
>   2. Is relative risk aversion constant across problem situations?
>   3. Does experience reduce variations in risk aversion?
>   4. Can education or simulated experience reduce variations in risk aversion?
>
> The 4th question is the one to be researched.

2. Importance of Research

> In the design of decision systems, a decision maker with a given risk aversion is usually assumed. But there is evidence (such as Allen, "Risk Aversion in Production Scheduling," *Journal of Business Research,* July 1971, pp. 475–490) that the decision models are less effective than one would hope because of variations in patterns of risk aversion. There is, therefore, a need to evaluate methods for reducing variations in risk aversion by a decision maker. Burnham states, "There is an urgent need to understand the risk aversion phenomenon and to find and evaluate mechanisms for altering risk aversion behavior if the new decision systems are to be effective."

3. Significant Prior Research

> There are a number of studies of risk aversion as determined by personality and environment. Hurst ("Constancy of Risk Aversion," *Journal of Decision Psychology,* January 1969, pp. 120–131) experimented with 10 college students and concluded that absolute risk aversion was affected by the problem, but the relative risk aversion evidenced by different subjects was not changed. Wadell ("Effect of Trauma on Risk Aversion," *Journal of Decision Psychology,* February 1970, pp. 5–14) ran experiments which suggest traumatic experience is effective in changing risk aversion for broad classes of related phenomena. No reported research has been found on the effect of education and simulated experience on reducing variations in risk aversion.

4. Possible Research Approach or Methodology

Five methodologies for research are possible. One or more may be used. 1-3 are proposed.

1. Use a group of students and measure variations in risk aversion behavior prior to taking the Decision Sciences course in Fall Quarter, immediately following the course in December, and 6 months after taking the course in May.
2. Use a group of inventory controllers taking a course in scientific inventory management. Measurement before, after, and 6 months after.
3. Use a group of students and measure the change in variability of risk aversion after using the inventory management decision simulator, which provides experience in handling uncertainty by means of decision rules.
4. Use a group of inventory controllers and measure change after use of inventory management decision simulator.
5. Observe changes in card playing behavior (Poker and Hearts) by students who have received instruction in assessing the probability of certain combinations of cards.

Instruments: An instrument to measure risk aversion variation would have to be constructed and validated. Perhaps it could be constructed from parts of existing personality tests, such as the Alison battery and the Jann test for objectivity.

The inventory management decision simulator is available. A data generator to produce the desired stimuli would need to be added.

6-1 cont'd.

5. Potential Outcomes of Research and Importance of Each

Outcomes are contributions in part of cases; others probably not.

1. Immediate Effect of Education

	Students	Controllers
Variability Reduced	Contribution	Contribution
Variability Increased	?	?
No Effect	No contribution	No contribution

2. 6–Month Effect of Education. Same as 1.

3. Effect of Simulated Experience

	Students Only
Variability Reduced	Contribution
Variability Increased	?
No Effect	No contribution

The increase in variability is difficult to interpret and is not as strong a contribution as reduction in variability, unless a theoretical basis for the result can be found.

6-1 cont'd. Topic analysis form (all references, etc., are hypothetical).

Problem, hypothesis, or question This states what the dissertation will deal with. If hypotheses are appropriate, they should be stated. If the type of topic is not amenable to statement as a hypothesis, then the problem or question should be clearly stated.

Importance of the research   This addresses the question of whether or not the research is important or significant enough to justify doing. If there is some statement by an authority as to need for this research, or if it can be demonstrated that this research is significant to a major activity, then this or related reasons should be concisely stated in a short paragraph. The importance of a dissertation need not be earth-shaking, but no dissertation should deal with a trivial or inconsequential topic.

Significant prior research   This part mentions the major preceding research. It need not be exhaustive when topics are being selected, but the student should make a quick investigation, taking perhaps ten to twenty hours, to look at the major research work on the topic.

The possible research approach or methodology   This section of the topic analysis is extremely important because it outlines how the student proposes to approach the research. Is it via questionnaire, simulation, data collection, measurement, or algorithm solution? The approach should be explained as precisely as possible but may still be in a very rough form. Alternative methodology should be included. Most doctoral candidates have taken a research methodology course which described alternative methodologies. Appendix II provides selected references which may be used to supplement the student's course knowledge.

The potential outcomes and importance of each   The contents of this section are vital to an assessment of the dissertation proposal. For each research approach, the different but possible outcomes should be described. For example, a topic analysis might propose a project to collect evidence by a questionnaire. Then the questionnaire results would be analyzed statistically to determine if there is a positive correlation between perceived behavior and the responses to questions. The potential outcomes might be:

   1.   A significant positive correlation demonstrating the relationship;

2. A significant negative correlation demonstrating the reverse of what was expected;

3. A lack of correlation (probably proving nothing);

4. An inability to obtain satisfactory responses on the questionnaire.

In this particular case, perhaps only one of the potential outcomes might be expected to result in an acceptable dissertation. But it may be possible to structure the data collection and analysis so that a negative correlation might also turn out to be acceptable.

The topic analysis has the objective of assisting the candidate in eliciting helpful comments and alternative suggestions. Therefore, if there are viable alternatives, these should be included (or prepared as a separate topic). Note in the sample shown in Figure 6-1 that several alternatives are suggested, and one is indicated as being preferable.

SELECTING AMONG THE ALTERNATIVE TOPICS

Some topics can be eliminated from further consideration because time or cost are too great. The dissertation advisor and committee may reject other topics as unsuitable. One topic may turn out to be far superior and end the selection process. However, if there are several topics to choose among, the selection should proceed by assessing for each topic the following two probabilities:

1. *The probability of successful completion* To assist in this assessment, make two lists for each topic.

   a. A list of the expected chapters in the dissertation

   b. A list of major activities required to do the dissertation together with time estimates for each

   If it is difficult or impossible to outline the dissertation and the steps to complete it, this indicates potential difficulty in completion. Students frequently indicate they will perform a simulation, build a prototype, establish an experiment. It is important to assess the difficulty of carrying out such activities. If it cannot be planned, it probably cannot be done.

2. *The probability of acceptance of the completed research as a dissertation* This consists of two sets of probabilities.

    a. The probability that each of the outcomes will make a contribution to knowledge

    b. The probability that the committee will accept each of the results as a contribution

There are, of course, other factors such as personal preference, personal standards of research quality, the dissertation as a basis for future work, and professional development.

The final decision is a personal one, but a student should be aware of the relative risks of various topics. A candidate may still choose a risky topic over a "safe" topic, but the choice should be made with an awareness of the risk.

The Proposal

The idea of the topic analysis was to make it short so that it would be feasible to prepare several for alternative topics. When one of these topics is finally chosen, the dissertation proposal should be prepared. It is an expansion of the topic analysis and will be used as a work plan for the dissertation. Whereas a topic analysis of two to four pages was adequate, a complete final proposal might contain ten to thirty pages. The structure of the proposal (with some idea of reasonable page length) is approximately as follows:

Section of Proposal	*Reasonable Page Length*
1. Summary	1 - 2
2. Hypothesis, problem, or question	1 - 3
3. Importance of topic	1 - 2
4. Prior research on topic	1 - 7

5. Research approach or research method-
   logy   2 - 8
6. Limitations and key assumptions   1 - 2
7. Contributions to knowledge (for each
   potential outcome, if there are more than
   one)   1 - 3
8. Descriptions of proposed chapters in dissertation   2 - 3

The *summary* section of the proposal contains one or two paragraphs summarizing what the dissertation project is to do and how it is to do it. The *hypothesis, problem, or question* section is similar to the same section in the topic analysis but is amplified and refined. The same holds true for the section on the *importance of the topic.*

The *prior research* section should be expanded over that which was included in the topic analysis. It should be more comprehensive because there should now be a search of all major sources of information. If there has been considerable prior work, it can be summarized. This section might consist of from one to five pages. Too many pages indicate a need for summarization, since this is the proposal, not the dissertation itself.

The *research approach or research methodology* section should be as explicit as possible. The data collection or experiment should be explained. If a questionnaire is to be used, for example, the questionnaire methodology should be explained, and perhaps examples of the major types of questions to be asked should be mentioned. Population and selection or sampling procedures should be outlined. If a simulation is to be used, the major elements of the simulation should be defined. If an experimental situation is to be used to collect data, there should be a description covering the subjects, the apparatus to be used, procedures to be followed, data to be collected, and the instruments to be used in data collection. Obviously, there are many unanswered questions. The idea is to sketch the research approach as clearly as possible. Major questions yet to be decided should be listed.

The *limitations or key assumptions* section is important because it defines the limits of the dissertation work. It is common for students to try to do too much, and the limitations and key assumptions section is useful in defining how much the student will undertake, and in describing key assumptions to govern the building of the model or conducting of the experiment. This should be very explicit—"The research will not . . . ."

The *contributions* section is similar to the section in the topic analysis and can be written in more detail.

The *chapter descriptions* are an attempt to further define the dissertation. Each chapter can be described in terms of its major headings or by a short paragraph describing what will be covered in that chapter. It should be as specific as possible, but since this is a proposal document, the chapter descriptions should be brief and highlight the structure rather than give much detail. Most dissertations follow a standard format consisting of the following chapters or sections:

1. *The introduction*   The general problem area, the specific problem, why the topic is important, research approach of the dissertation, limitations and key assumptions, and contribution to be made by the research are described.

2. *A description of what has been done in the past*   This is a rather complete survey of prior research. If prior research is very limited, this description might be combined with Chapter 1; if there is extensive prior research, the results might have to be divided into two or more chapters. The prior research review is normally an important section of the dissertation because the description of what has been done provides background to the research. It also documents the fact that the candidate's research is unique because the work of the dissertation has not been covered by prior research.

3. *A description of the research methodology* One or more chapters may be used to describe the research method. For example, the chapter(s) might describe a simulation, a data collection technique, a measurement technique, an experiment, or an historical method of analysis. In essence, this section describes how the research was conducted.

4. *The research results* The results of the chosen methodology are reported; the data are presented, the conceptual framework is described, the historical analysis is defined, or the comparative studies are explained.

5. *Analysis of the results* This may be included with prior chapters depending upon the type of dissertation. This is a key section because it explains the conclusions that can be drawn from the data and the implications of a theory.

6. *Summary and conclusions* The dissertation is summarized with emphasis upon the results obtained and the contribution made by these results. Suggestions for further research are also outlined.

With the general structure of a dissertation plus the characteristics of the specific dissertation in mind, the student is usually able to define the chapters of the dissertation. The chapter descriptions are frequently very useful in helping to focus on the objective of a completed, accepted dissertation.

The proposal is a plan for the student to follow. It also provides the dissertation committee with information by which they can approve or reject the project. Approval does not mean automatic approval of the dissertation. But if the proposal is explicit, the committee approval implies that when the proposed work is done properly and clearly documented in a dissertation, there is a high probability that the dissertation will be accepted. A well-done proposal, when accepted by the committee, forms a type of contract (in a personal rather than a legal sense) between the candidate and the committee.

Refining a Proposal

The first proposal is not usually the final proposal. There is a process of refining in which reviews, critical comments, and suggestions are incorporated into revised drafts which are reviewed. The end result of the review and rewriting (and perhaps starting over with a new proposal) is a complete, crisply defined proposal.

The process of moving from an idea for a dissertation to a concise, well-defined proposal is sometimes the most difficult task of the entire dissertation. It is not unusual for candidates to take six, eight, ten, or more months to get a topic defined. There is no simple recipe for approaching the process, but some hints may prove helpful.

NARROWING THE SCOPE

The point needs to be repeated—almost every student starts with a project that is too large. One way to narrow the dissertation topic is to attempt to subdivide it into more than one dissertation. The subdivisions are each analyzed as a topic. The result may be to choose only one of the subdivisions, and this will usually prove to be a smaller, more manageable topic. For example, a student who wished to study the writing of doctoral dissertations might start out with the topic: "An investigation of the Factors Affecting Completion of High Quality Doctoral Dissertations and a Proposed Method for Improving Performance." This can be subdivided into at least three topics, for example, the following:

1. An investigation into the time taken to complete dissertations
2. An investigation into the factors affecting the quality of a doctoral dissertation
3. An investigation into a systematic method for managing a doctoral dissertation with some results from a pilot application.

Note that by separating out three dissertations, the scope of each is much better defined and much more likely to be completed.

The student might also consider what the research is trying to accomplish—what he or she hopes to get as a result. If this is difficult to define, a useful technique is to imagine the dissertation is complete and the final chapter with summary and conclusions is being written. What will be the conclusions? What might be the main points of the results? By trying to draft the conclusions, the main thrust of the dissertation should become clearer and this will help to narrow the scope.

CLARIFYING THE PURPOSE OF THE RESEARCH

Students should try to avoid a "fishing" approach to research. A student who collects much data and then applies multiple regression techniques to "see what comes out" is not likely to be able to differentiate between spurious and real correlation or to have collected all relevant data. This example is perhaps obvious, but students who collect data or begin interviews without a clear idea of objectives are likely to commit the same fault.

One of the best ways to define the objectives of the research is by the statement of hypotheses which the research methodology will accept or reject. For example, the first of the previous examples of dissertation topics might be stated as a hypothesis that "time taken by candidates to complete doctoral dissertations is a function of: (list)." By listing the factors, the data collection methodology and analysis procedures can be related to the factors that are thought to be important. It is sometimes useful to introduce a competing theory rather than only defining null hypotheses based on a single theory.

Some topics are not amenable to hypotheses statements. For example, conceptual development and comparative analysis are not usually amenable to hypothesis statements. The third example of a topic was the investigation of a systematic dissertation management method and pilot study. Since this topic is difficult to state as a hypothesis, the research methodology can be clarified and defined by restating the topic in terms of a set of objectives for the research, such as the following:

1. To develop a useful approach for the use of doctoral candidates (approach will be synthesized from management theory and psychological theory)
2. To support the validity of the approach by reference to research and theory in management and psychology
3. To demonstrate feasibility of approach in a pilot study
4. To provide support (but not statistical evidence) for utility of approach by a pilot study

Note the fact that the student plans to build an approach (a model of the dissertation completion process) using accepted theory from other fields. Experimental and other evidence from these fields that have been reported in the literature will be used to support the fact that the conceptual structure is sound. The pilot study is very useful (although not always necessary) in demonstrating the feasibility of the approach. A small pilot study may also provide data suggesting the utility of the approach, but the sample is usually too small to be statistically significant.

CHECKING FEASIBILITY OF RESEARCH METHODOLOGY

Despite the advice to delay data collection until a proposal is prepared, there are some cases where some preliminary investigation is very desirable to check the feasibility of research. Some examples will illustrate such situations.

Case 1: The proposed dissertation research methodology is highly dependent on the use of a panel of experts. There should be some discussion with one or more experts during topic formulation in order to get some insight into the practicality of the technique and the probability of obtaining usable data.

Case 2: The proposed methodology involves the initiation of a prototype instructional program in the school. The success of the dissertation is dependent on a school's willingness to have a prototype program and the availability of persons to carry it out. There should be some preliminary investigation during the proposal writing stage to assess the probability of these conditions being satisfied for the research.

Case 3: The proposed methodology into the time taken for doctoral dissertations requires that a sample of recent doctorates and a sample of "all but dissertation" candidates, at varying stages of completion, be surveyed. This is dependent on locating the current address of these subjects. A preliminary investigation of the quality and availability of the university address files is important in assessing the feasibility of the methodology. A pretest of a proposed questionnaire might provide evidence on both the questionnaire and the address file.

The illustrations show that there are times when some preliminary investigation is required to get sufficient insight on the problem, the methodology, or the state of the data in order to be able to make a good proposal. In these cases, it is wise to draft the clearest proposal possible before conducting the investigations. After these investigations, revise the proposal. A first draft proposal will serve as a guide to the preliminary investigations.

EVALUATING FEASIBILITY VIA A SCENARIO

One method for testing feasibility is to write a short scenario, or outline, of the actions, activities, and responses that can be expected as the dissertation research proceeds through the crucial phases. Such a scenario may reveal some very important data collection or analysis steps which are difficult or impossible to perform. If a student cannot visualize a research scenario from the current point through to completion, it is likely that the research topic is not a good one.

PROPOSAL SEMINARS

Proposal seminars (either formal or informal) can subject the proposal to the ideas of a larger group. Such a presentation should be made as soon as a fairly complete proposal is written instead of waiting until the research work is well in progress. If the faculty have not provided such a review, the doctoral candidates in an area may wish to do this on an informal basis. A student may get so close to a problem that he or she cannot see it in perspective; a review session with faculty or other students may help to clarify the proposal. It is important that such seminars be supportive and helpful rather than a "mini exam," so that candidates will seek advice and constructive criticism. At one university, the proposal seminars became so critical of the research that candidates would not present a proposal until they were almost finished with the research. This negates the major benefit which should come from the seminar—to help the student evaluate (and further define) a proposed topic under investigation.

METHODS OF PRESENTING THE PROPOSED RESEARCH

The ways in which the proposed research is presented can often help define the dissertation proposal. Two examples will illustrate the method of presentation as a factor in clarifying the dissertation.

Example 1: Four researchers have done work with a population similar to that being proposed. The dissertation proposal needs to show the relationship of the prior research to the proposed research in

CHARACTERISTICS OF RESEARCH DESIGN

Researcher	Population	Sample Size	Experi-mental Method	Type of Reinforce-ment	Reinforce-ment Schedule
Allon & Michael	Hospital-ized schiz & mental defectives	19	2 phase baseline period treatment	Approval & ignoring	Intermit-tent on 1 to 3 intervals
Ayllon & Azrin	Hospital-ized chronic females	47	3 phase; contingent, non-con-tingent, and contingent	Tokens awarded to be ex-changed for goods	6 experi-ments each with differ-ent rein-forcement schedule
Atthowe & Krasner	Hospital-ized veterans 22 yr. median stay	60	3 phase: baseline, 3 mo. shaping, and 11 mo. treatment	Tokens and social approval	Contingent on behavior specified in advance
Panek	Same as Atthowe & Krasner		Compared common associates learning with token reinforce-ment and punish-ment		
Proposal	Day Treatment Center Veterans	73	2 phase; 2 week baseline and 8 wk. treatment	Tokens worth five cents	Contingent on behavior specified in advance

6-2.   An example research comparison table as a method of relating a research proposal to prior research in a field.

order to (1) define both the similarities and the differences, and (2) evaluate the potential contributions of the proposed research. These objectives can be achieved by presenting the past research and proposed research in a research comparison table (Figure 6-2).

Example 2: The proposal has a hypothesis that there will be changes in career development after the introduction of a career exploration unit in a tenth grade English class. The testing of the hypothesis hinges on the operational definition of "career maturity," as it relates to the particular classroom exercises. The table of expected research effects (Figure 6-3) was prepared to show which scales in a career maturity inventory might be expected to change because of the experimental intervention. The "X"

Career Maturity Inventory Scale	Effect of Classroom Exercises X = change expected O = no change expected	
	Self-Concept Exploration Topic	Satisfactions and Rewards of Work Topic
Attitude Scale		
a) Involvment in choice process	X	O
b) Orientation toward work	O	X
c) Preference for career choice	X	X
d) Independence in decision making	X	O
e) Conceptions of the choice process	X	X
Competence Test		
a) Knowing yourself	X	O
b) Knowing occupations	O	X
c) Choosing the job	X	X
d) Planning for the job	O	X
e) Problem solving ability	X	O

6-3. Example of table of expected research effects.

indicates where change in scale scores might be expected because of the classroom exercise. The "0" indicates no change is expected.

A CHECKLIST

The following checklist is not exhaustive, but it suggests useful questions a student should ask during a self-appraisal of the proposal.

1. Does the proposal have imagination?
2. Is the problem stated clearly?
   a. Are the hypotheses clear, unambiguous, and testable?
   b. If no hypotheses, are the objectives clearly stated? Can they be accomplished?
   c. Is the problem too large in scope?
3. Is the methodology feasible?
   a. Can data be collected?
   b. How will data be analyzed?
   c. Will the analysis allow the acceptance or rejection of the hypothesis?
   d. Is the population to be sampled overused? (Navajos must be tired of anthropologists, and *Fortune*'s 500 companies must be tired of surveys.)
4. What might the results of the analysis look like? (A useful technique in clarifying the proposal is to try to sketch the form of the tables or other results from the data analysis. The axes of graphs can be labeled and the probable shape of curves estimated. The expected results from correlation, factor analysis, or analysis of variance can be sketched.)
5. What are the consequences to the dissertation if —
   a. the experiment fails;
   b. data cannot be obtained (for each major item of data);

      c.   only a small amount of data exists;

      d.   the analysis is inconclusive;

      e.   the hypothesis is rejected or accepted?

6.   Can major research activities be listed?

7.   Can a time estimate be attached to each major activity?

8.   Is the dissertation trying to do too much?

9.   If yes to 8, what can be dropped or reduced to make the project of manageable dimensions?

10.   If the student will have to complete elsewhere (against good advice, but it does happen), is the dissertation portable; i.e., can it be completed away from the university?

CHAPTER 7

The Dissertation Time Schedule and Budget

While the proposal is being refined, the student should also prepare a time budget and time schedule. Students (and professors) tend to underestimate the time required for completing a dissertation. A formal, detailed estimating approach is likely to yield a better estimate than an overall estimate without any breakdown. All of the estimates use work hours or work months (of 175 work hours). These are converted into elapsed time by a separate computation, taking into account the percentage of time a student can work on the dissertation.

Standard Times

There are no standards for how long a dissertation should take.[1] Some estimates were presented in Chapter 2. These will be expanded in this chapter as bases for preparing a time schedule.

Table 7-1 presents the authors' estimates of the time required for doctoral dissertations. The basis for standard time is the estimated median time for doing a good dissertation if the student follows a systematic approach to the management of the

---

[1]There have been some studies of the time dimension. These studies note some variability in time taken. For example, dissertations for English departments take substantially longer than average. For a listing of books dealing with this subject, consult the bibliography.

TABLE 7-1. STANDARD TIMES FOR DISSERTATION

	Standard	Range Low	High
Page length (see Figure 2-1)	225	100	450
Total effective work months from topic search to acceptance	14	10	21
Breakdown: (work months)			
Topic search and proposal	3	1	8
Search prior research	1	1	3
Research and analysis activity	5	4	12
Writing, editing, and proofing	5	3	12
Elapsed time taking into account delays (with full-time work on dissertation)			
From topic search to acceptance	16	12	29
From approved proposal to acceptance	12	10	24

*Based on estimates by authors.

dissertation project. This estimate underlies many of the other estimates presented in this chapter. The low and high range are estimated to include 90 percent of all dissertations.

There are a number of variables that affect these estimates. Some of these are listed; the student must assess how such factors will affect personal estimates of completion.

Variable	Comments
Discipline by student (ability to stick to project)	Good discipline reduces time.
Quality of dissertation	Standard estimate assumes good quality (say 70 to 85 percentile on a subjective

	scale of quality). If average quality (50th percentile) is assumed, time *may* be reduced, but this does not always follow.
Hours devoted per month	Standard hours in a month are 175. Many students spent more than this on the dissertation; others think they do but don't.
Random events	The baby becomes ill, the house burns down, there are university riots, someone has written the computer analysis needed, and other similar events may occur.
Advisor response time	Can be quite variable for same advisor.
Job interviews and moving to a new job	Often necessary but very disruptive.
Predissertation development activities	A student who selects a topic early and follows the development activities outlined in Chapter 4 may be able to reduce the standard elapsed time (but not necessarily the time spent). Many acivities will have been done prior to formally beginning the dissertation in connection with course work, etc.

The reason for being quite specific in time estimates, even at the risk of error, is that students frequently have very unrealistic ideas of the time required for a dissertation. Most think it will take less time than it does, but every so often a student starts talking about a four-year project. Advisors are naturally reluctant to say how long it takes to do a dissertation for fear of misleading a candidate. These estimates may provide the basis for discussion in doctoral research seminars where recently completed candidates may report their times and comment on the standard times.

Preparing the Time Estimate

There are several ways to approach a time estimate. One method, illustrated in Figure 7-1, requires the student to—

1. define the expected dissertation structure (major chapters and sections within chapters as being prepared for the proposal);
2. estimate the page length by chapter;
3. estimate tasks;
4. estimate times by task;
5. estimate elapsed time.

The time estimate form assumes it is being prepared after the topic has been selected and during the refining of the proposal. The following discussion will follow the format of the estimating form in Figure 7-1.

REFINING DISSERTATION STRUCTURE

The student is left somewhat on his or her own for this section but a few guidelines expressed in work hours may be helpful.

Range in Work hours	Low	High
Preparation of revised proposal	50	250
Detailed outline of dissertation	10	50

RESEARCH ACTIVITIES

	Estimated Work Hours
Examination of supporting literature (use 5-6 hours per 100 pages)	_____
Preparing instrument for collecting data (questionnaire, simulation, or experiment)	_____
Testing instrument for collecting data	_____
Collecting data (running experiment, doing question- naires, etc.)	_____
Data analysis (including all preparation for analysis)	_____
Developing concepts and theories	_____
Analysis of results	_____
Other	_____
Total	_____

WRITING, EDITING, REWRITING, AND PROOFREADING

Chapter	Approximate Title	Est. Pages	Work Hours Per Page Std. Est.	Rev. Est.	Work Hours per Chapter
_____	_____	____	4	____	_____
_____	_____	____	4	____	_____
_____	_____	____	4	____	_____
_____	_____	____	4	____	_____
_____	_____	____	4	____	_____
_____	_____	____	4	____	_____
_____	_____	____	4	____	_____
	Summary and conclusions	____	8	____	_____
	Bibliography	____	6	____	_____
	Appendices	____	–	____	_____
	Total				_____

7-1.

IDENTIFICATION

Student _____ Advisor _____

Date of estimate _____

Title or description of proposed dissertation:

REFINING OF DISSERTATION STRUCTURE

	Student Estimate in Work Hours
Preparation of revised proposal	_____
Detailed outline of dissertation	_____
Other	_____
Total	[_____]

FURTHER SEARCH OF LITERATURE FOR PRIOR RESEARCH

Sources to be Searched	Est. No. to be Searched	Standard Estimate	Student Estimate	Total Work Hours
		Hours for Each		
Journal articles	_____	1.0	_____	_____
Books	_____	10.0	_____	_____
Dissertations	_____	10.0	_____	_____
Government documents	_____	3.0	_____	_____
Other (documents, computer searches)	_____		_____	_____
		Total	[_____]	

7-1 cont'd.

TOTAL ESTIMATED WORKHOURS

Refining of dissertation structure _____

Further search of literature for prior research _____

Research activities _____

Writing, editing, rewriting and proofing _____

Total work hours [_____]

ESTIMATED COMPLETION DATE

	Month	Year
Starting date for completion estimate	____	____

Working time in elapsed months

$$\left(\frac{\text{Total estimated work hours}}{175} \right) \left(\frac{1}{\substack{\text{Percent of time de-} \\ \text{voted to thesis}}} \right) \quad \underline{\quad}$$

Estimated completion time (no delays)   ____ ____

Delays expected: Months

     Data collection delays   _____

     Data analysis delays   _____

     Chapter reading delays   _____

     Final reading delays   _____

     Typing and printing delays   _____

     Other delays   _____   _____

Estimated final completion date
(ready for defense)   [_____]

7-1 cont'd. Time estimate for completing doctoral dissertation using chapter and task estimates.

FURTHER SEARCH OF LITERATURE FOR PRIOR RESEARCH

The literature search estimate here is the one to establish the originality of the research being performed. It takes longer to search a book than an article. Some standard times are shown but the student should apply individualized estimates. The same approach may be used to estimate the literature review time connected with research activities.

RESEARCH ACTIVITIES

Different research activities are listed but the student should define the main research tasks connected with the dissertation and estimate the time required for each. The total time in work hours will probably fall in the 700 to 1400 work-hour range.

WRITING, EDITING, REWRITING, AND PROOFREADING

This is an area where students consistently underestimate the time required to document the research. The standard estimate is four hours per double-spaced typewritten page of final manuscript. The student might remember doing a five-page paper in one evening and applies that time estimate, but it is not sufficient. In fact, many students require more than four hours per page. The summary and conclusions usually must be rewritten several times, so the standard time for the final chapter is double, or eight hours per page. The bibliography is time consuming to set up and proofread, so a six-hour-per-page estimate is used. Appendices may include computer printouts, copies of questionnaires, letters used in data collection, and tests used. These still take time to include, but there is no way to establish a standard estimate.

Scheduling Activities

After preparing a gross time budget, the activities should be sequenced through time. This can be somewhat rough but should be complete. Figure 7-2 shows a sample format. This method is often termed a Gantt chart. Using the Gantt chart of activities, major review points should then be planned. This will be important in working with the advisor and the committee. Figure 7-3 is a sample format for critical review dates.

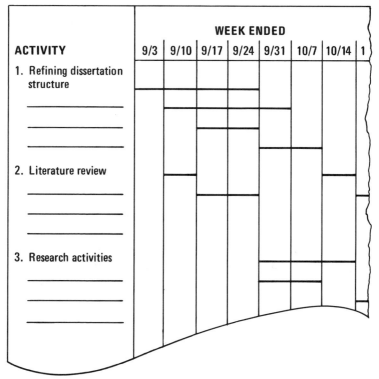

7-2. Scheduling of dissertation activities (Gantt chart).

Student _____

CRITICAL REVIEW DATES

Review Activity	Review by	Earliest Date	Latest Date	Planned Date
Review of final proposal	Committee	_____	_____	_____
Review of methodology or approach	Advisor et. al.	_____	_____	_____
Review of questionnaire and sampling plan	Committee	_____	_____	_____
Review of test sample results	Advisor	_____	_____	_____
Review of revised sampling	Committee	_____	_____	_____
Review of Chapter 1 and 2	Advisor	_____	_____	_____

7-3.   Schedule of critical review dates.

If several activities are linked together so that completion of one is dependent upon the completion of one or more others, they are said to form a "critical path." In this case, the student might wish to make a very simple critical path analysis (see literature on critical path, CPM, or PERT such as F. K. Levy, G. L. Thompson, and J. D. Weist, "The ABC's of the Critical Path Method," *Harvard Business Review,* September-October 1963).

Reminder

The important concept is realistic planning and this must depend on realistic time estimates. The best estimates are usually made by breaking down the activities into small tasks and combining these estimates. The standard estimates should provide a check for individual estimates. A student who arrives at a six-month estimate may be very fortunate; more likely he or she is a poor estimator.

A student should not be dissuaded from making time estimates because there is a particular task that cannot be estimated. Estimate the other activities and then include a pessimistic, optimistic, and best estimate for the hard-to-project activity. It is better to have an imprecise estimate than no estimate at all.

A last point is that different subject fields have different modal times (the most common time students take to complete). If the modal time is twenty-five months instead of fourteen, this may reflect requirements in the area, or it may merely reflect dilatory work habits that students in the area have adopted because others before them did it that way.

A Dissertation Budget

Candidates are frequently surprised at the typing, copying, and binding costs required to complete the dissertation. Where a candidate has a grant for dissertation research, the final costs are frequently not covered. A dissertation budget should be prepared so these expenditures can be planned.

EXPENDITURES DURING RESEARCH WRITING

These expenditures will vary considerably depending on the type of research being performed. Examples are as follows:

Expenses of experiment (instruments, supplies, incentives, rewards, meals, snacks, etc.)

Postage

Telephone

Copies (dissertations, articles, books, etc., needed for literature review, etc.)

Keypunching or other data conversion expenses preparatory to computer analysis

Computer time and storage

Typing and reproduction of materials used in research

Typing and reproduction of material provided to committee

EXPENDITURES FOR READING AND FINAL APPROVAL PROCESS

	Example Expense (Based on 225 Pages)
Typing of draft copies for committee to read:	
(a) First draft (75¢/page)	$170
(b) Reader draft ($1.00/page)	225
Reproduction of draft for readers (approximately 5 copies at 6¢/page)	80
Typing of final copy ($1.00/page)	225
Reproduction of required copies (committee, university, etc.—approximately 10 copies at 6¢/page)	135
Binding of copies (approximately 10 copies at $10.00 each)	100
Other fees	65
TOTAL	$1,000

Typing costs vary from school to school, but a reasonable estimate (based on 1978 prices) is 75¢ per double-spaced page, typed from relatively clean copy. Tables and bibliography will be two to four times the normal page rate. An overall estimate for final typing of the entire dissertation is $1.00 per page. Drafts may often be obtained at a lower rate. Copying can often be purchased at less than 6¢ per page by shopping around.

These examples of costs are only illustrative and may, of course, vary considerably for different candidates. The point is that the final expenses are not trivial and need to be included in a plan.

CHAPTER 8

Working with an Advisor and a Dissertation Committee

The advisor is a crucial figure in the completion of a dissertation. The university entrusts the advisor with considerable power and responsibility in the dissertation acceptance process. The committee members are also important but less so than the advisor. The view of this chapter is that the advisor and committee have the responsibility of assisting the candidate; the student has the responsibility of presenting material in order to effectively use the scarce advisor and committee resource. This chapter explores procedures the student can follow to help make interaction with the advisor and committee effective. Problems can arise in this relationship. Students may get so involved in their research problem that they forget advisors are human beings. The chapter explores typical situations and possible solutions.

Aids to Effective Interaction with an Advisor and a Committee

The student should recognize that there are many demands on the advisor for time and attention, and there frequently are inter-

Candidate: Clark G. Flint   *Date of Meeting:* Oct. 16, 1977

Summary of Meeting with PH.D. Committee

In attendance: R. G. Smith, Advisor
John Hoffmann
Gary Gray

Absent: William Jones

1. **Review of Revised Outline of Chapter One**
   The committee expressed agreement with the revised outline. Professor Gray asked that the section on ethnic foundations of the problem be expanded to include the recent research by Maxwell and Pawlofski. This was agreed upon.

2. **Review of Proposed Data Collection Procedure**
   The proposed method of paired samples was approved. After reviewing the computations of sample size, the committee suggested that a sample size of 100 instead of 150 would be sufficient. The final decision will await the results of a pretest of a sample of 10.

3. **Review of Revised Dissertation Schedule**
   The revised schedule, calling for final reading of the first draft in July, was discussed. Professor Hoffmann indicated a change in plans makes a July reading not feasible, but he will be able to read it in the first week of August. The schedule was therefore revised to a faculty return of first draft manuscript by August 9.

4. **Next Meeting and Other Reviews**
   a. A sampling plan review with Professor Euwe of the statistics department has been scheduled for November by the candidate.
   b. A review of the experimental procedures prior to the pretest is scheduled with Professor Smith on November 8.
   c. The pretest will be conducted November 12-13. A written report of the pretest will be distributed on November 21.
   d. The committee agreed to review the results of the pretest on November 28 at 2:00 p.m. in the 6th floor conference room. The meeting is planned for about 1 hour.

8-1. Report of committee meeting.

ruptions which keep the advisor from devoting attention to the candidate. The candidate's problem is usually how to improve the probability of a timely and helpful response from the advisor. The suggested method consists of written notes, outlines, issue summaries, scheduled times for meetings, and meeting agendas.

1. *Provide written notes of meetings.* When meeting with the committee, the candidate should make notes. Immediately after the meeting he or she should write up these notes, summarizing what was talked about and any conclusions that were reached. The candidate should keep a file of the notes and provide copies of all notes to the advisor and, perhaps, to the committe, if relevant. If there have been a number of quick "question and answer" contacts with the committee, the candidate may wish to summarize the significant ones every two weeks

---

Candidate: Clark G. Flint   *Date:* November 1, 1977

Summary of Sampling Plan Review

A sampling plan review was held with Professor Euwe of the statistics department. Professor Euwe has had prior experience with this type of problem.

Professor Euwe agreed to the general procedure but expressed reservations about the adequacy of a sample size of 100 for discriminating the effects of cultural background. He reserved judgment until the pretest results.

He suggested that the statistics department "Cross Cultural Analysis Program" would provide an appropriate computer analysis of the data.

I have examined the program documentation, and it provides all analysis we have agreed upon except the h index which I will program separately.

8-2. Note summarizing significant discussion.

or month. The rule is that the candidate should take the responsibility for documenting the decisions and actions communicated by the advisor and the committee. Two examples of notes are included—one from a formal meeting of a committee (Figure 8-1) and the other, a note on sampling procedure agreed to by the committee member with the highest competence in the area of sampling (Figure 8-2).

2. *Provide outlines and issue summaries with each batch of materials the committee is asked to read.* A candidate hands an advisor a fifty-page manuscript to read with no outline and no indication of what issues are important. It is understandable that the professor puts off getting to it. A better approach is to provide the following set of materials:

a. *A transmittal note* This lists the materials being given and a gentle reminder of the date by which the advisor or committee have agreed to return comments. (See Figure 8-3.)

b. *Issue summary* A short statement tells the contents of the batch of materials and gives a short descrip-

---

Student: Clark G. Flint   *Date:* January 15, 1978

TO: Dissertation Committee: Smith, Hoffman, Gray and Jones

Attached is the draft of Chapter 2 for your review and comments. The committee agreed upon January 31 as the date for comments to be returned. It would be most helpful to me if I could have your comments by that date. I would appreciate having your comments on some ideas listed on an attached issue summary.

8-3. Transmittal memo.

Student: Clark G. Flint   *Date:* January 2, 1978

Issue Summary for Chapter 2

This chapter discusses past research on the influence of cultural background on decision-making style. Important issues to be noted in the chapter are:

1. Cultural definition is defined. Note that I have not included the Murphy factors for reasons described in the chapter. Do you have comments?
2. The research of O'Neil and Elwin is rejected. Because of its lack of control, the results are considered to be dubious. Do you agree with this rejection?

8-4. Issue summary.

tion of each issue (or area in material) to which the reader should direct attention or for which the the candidate would especially like comments. (See Figure 8-4.)

c. *Outline of each chapter* These outline the major headings. If only one or two chapters are being provided, it is helpful to attach the outline of all chapters, so the reader can keep the material received in context. (See Figure 8-5.)

d. *The material to be read* This should always be double spaced and typed. The candidate should keep a control copy and the readers should write notes on their copy.

3. *Schedule meetings.* Plan ahead and schedule the necessary meetings. A schedule for the dissertation work and a schedule of critical reviews (described previously) should assist the candidate and the advisor in deciding on the meetings to schedule. Distribute materials at least a week

Chapter 2

**A Review of Past Research on Influence
of Cultural Background on Decision-Making Style**

DEFINITIONS

Decision-Making Style

Cultural Background

RESEARCH INTO DECISION-MAKING STYLE

The Miller-Kontel Study — 1938

The Elmoore Study — 1961

The Jones Study — 1973

A Synthesis of Findings

*RESEARCH ON INFLUENCE OF CULTURAL
BACKGROUND ON DECISION-MAKING*

8-5.   Chapter outline.

before (and longer if a large number of pages). Send a
separate reminder notice of the meeting. Arrange well
in advance for a place to hold the meeting if this is a
problem. A good policy is to schedule the next meeting
at the conclusion of the current meeting, since there
can be a group discussion and resolution of conflicts
in schedules.

4. *Provide action agendas for meeting.* The candidate's advisor acts as chairman of the meeting, but the candidate
should discuss with the advisor whether or not a proposed draft agenda would be useful. Or the student may

prefer to be less formal and merely discuss meeting objectives. However, an agenda should still be prepared, either by the student or by the advisor. After the advisor approves the agenda, it should be sent along with the reminder notice to those who are to attend. The agenda should describe each point to be discussed and decisions, if any, to be made (Figure 8-6).

5. *Provide written responses and periodic progress reports.* If a committee member asks a question that the candidate cannot answer immediately, but for which he or she agrees to provide an answer later, the answer should be written and sent (keeping a copy for his or her file). The file of reports, agendas, and questions forms a partial diary of the candidate's activity.

AGENDA

CLARK G. FLINT DISSERTATION MEETING

November 8, 1977

3:15 p.m. in BA 6th Floor Seminar Room

1. Discussion of Chapter 3. Specific points to discuss are:

   a. Sampling plan

   b. Questionnaire, especially part II

   c. Problem of analysis of comments

2. Report of computer program to be used in analysis

8-6. Agenda for meeting of committee.

A periodic written progress report is useful if the candidate is not meeting regularly with the committee. For example, if a student leaves the university or the professor goes on short-term leave so that there is a lack of personal contact, a regular (monthly or bi-monthly) report is desirable. It is frustrating to have an advisee who is supposed to be working on a dissertation but who never reports in. Even a short half-page summary is better than no report.

Advisor and Committee Problems and Suggested Solutions

Even if a candidate approaches the advisor/committee relationship as described, there can be problems. No one can advise about these matters in advance, but some ideas may help a candidate if one of these problems occurs.

1. *The advisor goes on leave, goes to another university, takes a non-university position, or dies.* The regulations of the university will govern in each case, but a good dissertation file will assist in making a change when an advisor dies or leaves the university. If the candidate has followed a well-planned and well-documented dissertation stragety, one of the other members of the committee will probably be willing to take over. Or another member of the department may be asked to serve. A more sensitive situation arises when the advisor goes on leave. Often another member of the committee can serve as temporary advisor until the advisor returns. If, however, the advisor is the key person affecting the completion of the dissertation (and he or she is agreeable), the candidate may wish to follow him or her to the new location. When counting the cost of such an action, the student must also count the cost of a delay in the dissertation. In most

cases, however, the advisor role can be taken over by another. The current advisor should advise as to a replacement. Before a change is made, the student should frankly discuss with both the current advisor and the proposed replacement, who the advisor will be in the event the current advisor should return before the thesis is complete.

Many universities allow faculty members who go to another unversity to continue to act as advisors for candidates in process. Again, the decision to keep the old advisor or to get a new one depends on how critical the advisor is to the success of the dissertation and on the stage of the dissertation. If the dissertation is almost finished, the current advisor should be used; if just begun, a new advisor should probably be sought.

2. *One of the committee goes on leave.* The problem is similar to that of an advisor, except the advisor will assist in making a decision on committee replacement.

3. *The advisor or committee members will not read the drafts.* A common complaint by students is that faculty will not read prepared drafts. But students frequently make it difficult. Contrast the following two approaches and consider which is most likely to yield results.

Typical: Student suddenly appears with drafts. No chapter outlines or issue lists. Professor feels as if the draft will require hours of concentrated time to read and comment. It is difficult to find such a large block of time.

Better: Student has provided advance notice of material to be read, and committee have agreed on dates for return of material. Chapters have outlines and issue lists, so that the professor may segment the task of review.

In the case of an advisor who does not read the drafts, it is sometimes useful to try to get him to make a commitment as to a date when the draft will be read and request that he schedule a meeting of the committee to discuss the drafts. If this is not an appropriate strategy, the best tact is to ask for the best estimate of completion and return on that date. Keep repeating the process. Meanwhile, keep working. A well-defined dissertation will allow such parallel development.

If a committee member delays excessively in reading a draft, the advisor may assist. If there is an outline and an issue summary, the student may suggest a verbal discussion with the committee member of the points on the issue list.

4. *The advisor becomes intransigent or obstructionistic.* Fortunately, it doesn't happen often. In most cases, it is probably best for the student to talk privately with him and express his concerns. One should state feelings, but not accuse. It promotes better, freer discussion to say "I feel that you no longer think I can complete the dissertation." The advisor may be reacting negatively to some of the student's behavior. The student may have been discourteous or there may have been an honest difference about the research. If the discussion does not resolve the issue, the student can wait a little to see if things work out. If the problem continues, the student should explore whether or not the advisor wishes to continue. If the professor wishes to be released as an advisor, the student should select a new advisor; if not, the student must try to work it out again. A student may get

some help from others on the committee or other faculty, but this is generally the last resort rather than the first action.

5. *One of the committee becomes intransigent or obstructionistic.* The advisor is usually the key, but first a talk with the committee person, expressing fears and asking if there is something that should be changed, may be in order. It is generally easier to change committee members than an advisor, but it is far better to have the member request the change (on the basis of work load, change in interest for dissertation) than for a change to be forced.

6. *Someone else publishes the same research the student is doing.* This is rarely a problem in the social sciences. Two people who work on the same topic, but employ different methodology, can generally both claim a contribution. However, it may present some problems. The student should examine carefully what the other researcher has done and note differences in purpose, scope, and methodology. Look for the unanswered questions that the other researcher has not explored. Generally, with a little extra work, the student can add to and extend what has been done. Probably only one-fourth or one-fifth of the total dissertation time is connected with the key "contribution" factors, so even a complete duplication, requiring restructuring of the contribution elements, is not the same as starting over. The danger of such duplication is reduced by timely completion. It is the person who spends five years on a dissertation who is generally caught by duplication.

7. *The dissertation is rejected.* If the committee decision or the final oral result in a rejection of the dissertation, what then? If the student has been following a suitable

schedule of reviews, it is unlikely the committee will reject the dissertation. Rather, they are likely to suggest modifications. Tired and worn-out as the candidate may feel at this point, he or she should respond to the requests, and the dissertation will generally be accepted. It is useful to get criticisms that are expressed in terms of what needs to be done. Professorial courtesy will generally allow committee members to suggest minor modifications without objection from other members. But if such suggestion(s) will present a real problem, it is appropriate for the student to ask if the suggested work is necessary for the acceptance of the dissertation. The committee members will often make suggestions not only for revision of the dissertation but also suggestions for future work on the topic after acceptance of the dissertation. A suggestion involving considerable research will often fit into the future work category.

CHAPTER 9

Management of Dissertation Activities

Prior chapters have described how to select an advisor and committee, select a topic, prepare a proposal, and work with an advisor and committee. This chapter will describe the management of the individual dissertation activities. Emphasis will be on the management of activities that are general to most dissertations. The chapter will, therefore, not cover specific methodology considerations.

Research Records

The dissertation is a major project extending over a considerable period of time, so accurate and complete records need to be·maintained. At the time a student gets an idea or reads something in a journal, he or she may think that it need not be recorded—"I will remember it"—but the result is that many good ideas are lost, and many journal citations have to be found again. Some suggestions on research records are an investigator's journal and a coding and filing system.

THE INVESTIGATOR'S JOURNAL

The candidate should keep a diary or journal of research investigations. This can be a loose-leaf notebook, but the bound type of journal, commonly used by scientific investigators, might be more serviceable. Notes should be made of work performed, of decisions made, and of suggestions made by the advisor or committee members. These notes and suggestions will form the basis for some of the written communications with the advisor and the committee described in the previous chapter. However, if any questions arise about the summaries, the original notes are contained in the investigator's journal. The investigator's journal thus forms a chronological diary and record of work that has been performed and ideas, suggestions, and comments that are important to the dissertation.

A CODING AND FILING SYSTEM

Almost immediately, the candidate will be faced with the task of coding and filing information that accumulates. A logical system for coding and filing is by using major subtopics within the dissertation. For example, if the dissertation consists of six chapters and there are, within these chapters, twenty major subtitles, each of these subtitles can be the basis for classification of references, ideas, and other information as data is collected. A separate section of a notebook or a file folder may be used for each of these sections. Each idea, quotation, or data analysis is coded according to the section under which it falls. Usually it is a wise idea to have a general section for each chapter for the coding of information which does not seem to come under any of the subtopics, but is relevant to the chapter as a whole. The information collected should clearly be labeled as to source and the date it was obtained. A reference date is especially important for information obtained from personal interviews. Journal references should be complete.

It is wise for the student to decide immediately on a bibliographic and reference style. The exact style is not important.

It is more significant to decide on a single style. Many universities specify a style manual or specify one of several style manuals as acceptable (see Appendix II). Select one of the style manuals and follow the reference format. Putting all bibliographic references in the selected standard format will insure that all necessary bibliographic reference information is obtained. Also it will not be necessary to rearrange the references when dissertation drafts are written.

One copy of each draft prepared should be maintained in a file. As early drafts are revised, rewritten, and changed, it is sometimes useful to be able to return to the original which was the basis for the revision. The file represents a chronological record of the progress of the dissertation effort. There is one other important reason for having such a file. It is possible to lose drafts of dissertation chapters—briefcases are lost, or the mail does not get through. Whenever a university building burns there is always the story of professor X or student Y whose entire work of several years has been destroyed in the fire. Therefore, a candidate should always preserve one copy of each draft which has been written, preferably in a place separate from the rest of the records. Then, in the case of fire or any other disaster, the entire work is not lost. This happens infrequently, but the cost of a backup file is not substantial, and the peace of mind is probably worth the cost. The chronological file, if stored in a separate location, can be the backup file.

Planning and Control of Daily Work

One of the principles for doing work such as a dissertation is to provide structure for the work. Since structured work generally takes precedence over unstructured work, the management task is to put enough structure into the dissertation activity that it assumes a priority over other less important activities. Some suggestions are to begin each week with a planning hour and establish tasks for the week, estimating times for each of the tasks. A larger number of tasks than can actually be completed should be outlined, putting priority on their completion. The extra tasks function as alternatives; they can be begun if the planned task cannot be completed for some reason. At the next planning session, the actual times can be compared to the estimated times, and decisions can be made as to effectiveness of work and as to the amount of time to be allowed for activities in the coming week.

Writing the Dissertation Drafts

Writing activity is somewhat personal, but certain approaches seem to be very successful. The student should decide upon a format for chapter headings, subheadings, and further subdivisions. These are usually included in a manul of style. The exact format is not nearly as important as selecting a pattern and following it consistently.

The chapter or subchapter to be written should be outlined in detail before writing begins. This will result in much more coherent and cohesive writing. Sections should be drafted as soon as possible. Dissertation writing should be viewed as an iterative process, and a chapter, consisting of four subsections, may be written a section at a time, as the material for each of the subsections has been obtained. This will result in a somewhat choppy chapter, but the editing activity is usually much less difficult than the original composition. References should be included in the original draft in a proper form.

A first draft will need to be edited and refined. One approach that works quite well is to read an entire chapter or major subsection, and then decide if the organization appears to be acceptable. If so, the chapter is edited for individual sentence structure, style, and content. If not, a new outline is prepared, and the chapter is reorganized. Then it is edited to smooth out the roughness which comes from reorganization.

Obtaining Methodological Assistance

Candidates frequently need assistance with such matters as statistical analyis, computer processing, or questionnaire design. It is always useful to have a member of the committee who will assist in reviewing the candidate's plans. Some universities provide special groups to assist doctoral candidates and others in such matters as statistics and computer processing. Candidates may also find other students who have special competence and who are willing to help if the amount of assistance required is reasonable.

There are a number of sets of computer programs to do statistical processing. Some of the more common packages are listed in Appendix III. Most university computing centers have consultants who will assist in the use of the statistical packages, and the candidate should make use of this source of advice. Advice should be sought in such a way that the probability of getting correct advice is high. Many candidates go to the software consultant and mumble something about needing some statistical analysis done. A likely response might be "There's a manual at the bookstore." Such advice is not very helpful. The student should prepare for seeking processing advice by preparing a description of the problem, the data that are available, the form of the data, the amount and the type of analysis required.

In utilizing computer processing, the candidate should make sure the program being used correctly does what is desired. Documentation provided for users of the program should be read carefully. Particular attention should be paid to controls which will assure the student that all of the data has been processed in the intended way. For example, the program should provide a count of the number of records being used by the program. If this is not provided as part of the standard output from the program, the candidate should seek to have this provided in a supplementary manner.

It is probably worthwhile for any candidate using a computer to obtain a rudimentary working knowledge of a high-level computer language such as FORTRAN in which most software packages are written. This enhances his or her ability to understand the advice being given. A rudimentary working knowledge in a high-level computer language can be obtained in ten to twenty hours; an elementary-level proficiency may take twenty to forty-five hours, depending on the language.

Candidates frequently design their questionnaires and data collection forms without any regard to the problems of keypunching the data into cards. This may present substantial difficulties and introduce errors. If the candidate does not have prior experience, he or she is well advised, prior to completing the questionnaire or data collection design, to examine the process by which cards are punched and discuss the punching of data with the person who will arrange for keypunching. The candidate should always take steps to control the quality of the input data and the quality of keypunching. As a minimum, a listing of input data should be examined and tested for errors. See Appendix III for ten questions to consider in data preparation, using punched cards.

A candidate should be able to discuss the method of determining that the results of the computer analysis were correct. Results can be tested to check if they are reasonable, or a problem can be run in more than one way, to provide a cross check of the results. Most computer statistical packages that are frequently used are correct, but there have been sufficient instances of incorrect computer programs that the candidate should carefully evaluate the correctness of the processing.

Coping with Problems

A dissertation which is planned to be written over a period of one and one-half or more years will never be done without the occurrence of some problems. One area of concern is personal health and family relationships; the other area relates to coping with failure situations.

PERSONAL HEALTH AND FAMILY RELATIONSHIPS

Doing a dissertation can be a terrible grind, and there is considerable pressure on candidates to work long hours. However, this can lead to poor health and exhaustion so that the candidate is not alert enough to do a good job. A work pattern should be established, based on a plan of work for each week. However, there should also be times for recreation. This is especially important should there be a wife, husband, or children involved. Students frequently mention the strain that the dissertation causes regarding spouse and family. However, one of the most difficult problems, apparently, is not the fact that the candidate is working long hours but that the spouse and family feel that there is no time which belongs to them. Advice which seems to have been quite successful suggests that the candidate should block out certain times during the week for family activities. For example, he or she may identify one evening, from 5 to 8 p.m., for family activities with the children. The candidate might agree with his or her spouse that Friday and Saturday nights are available for social activities with friends and that part or all of Sunday will be kept free for activities appropriate to their situation. Such a plan not only improves the mental and physical health of the candidate, but it is likely to keep the family relationships more healthy.

THE BEST LAID PLANS . . . OR COPING WITH
FAILURE SITUATIONS

This manual has been written from the view that a planned systematic approach to the dissertation will assist a candidate avoid most of the pitfalls and difficulties encountered in completing the dissertation. Our experience is that even well-planned projects sometimes go awry. This happens for many reasons, some of which are out of the control of the candidate. We have attempted to identify some of these below with some suggestions for coping with them.

1. *The project does not go as planned.* Research leads one into unknown areas. Even when one is familiar with existing research and related literature, and when one attempts to anticipate the problems and difficulties in collecting data, judgments can be in error, or new directions can become more fruitful. When this happens, it is important to reconsider prior decisions to see at which point(s) the research needs to be redirected. For example, one student had developed a carefully designed study of the effects of a communications training program. The plan was to test the program in the field. After several months of planning, checking detail, and doing a pilot run, a block was encountered in persuading actual clients to consent to participate in the research. A strong incentive was needed or it would be necessary to move the research back into the laboratory. Since there were no funds available for incentive, the decision was made to make a "laboratory test" offering the communications training program free in exchange for the research data. Fortunately, the data being collected were sufficiently different from those previously collected so that it was worthwhile to complete the research.

2. *Momentum is lost.* The graduate experience makes many demands. A student is often married, has family obligations,

works part time, and attempts to maintain a normal social life. With all of this, the thesis can be easily set aside and let go for a period. When this happens, the data get rusty, procedures are interrupted, or the writing becomes stale. Then the task is especially difficult to get "back to." Perhaps the most important remedy in such cases is a good dose of honesty. Advisors are in a difficult position, not wanting to take over responsibility for the success of the project, yet not wanting the student to fail. Most wait patiently, gently prod and encourage, but must rely on the student's initiative to become active again. If the student can confront himself with his responsibility and admit he needs extra help in getting started, the advisor can usually work out a plan for systematic checks until the student has assumed full responsibility again.

3. *Discouragement and depression.* Graduate students are *people.* They are subject to the same range of emotions, fears and joys, that other experience. Students sometimes get discouraged or depressed, and that interrupts progress on the dissertation. There are good reasons for this. As we have emphasized, the project is a large one requiring from one to two years to complete. The candidate is usually working alone. The data are often complex and sometimes confusing. The process can become downright drudgery at times, particularly during the analysis and writing stages. What was to be a creative contribution to the field turns out to be, at certain times, routine, hard work. Because of lack of experience and accurate information the student may feel all alone, overwhelmed and incompetent to complete the work. As the data are collected the student may fear that the results will not confirm the hypotheses. In general, there is very little positive reinforcement to keep the project moving. It is quite natural for depression to set in if these periods are not realistically anticipated and planned for.

Acknowledging these possibilities often allows a candidate to plan his life to include activities that are personally rewarding and, thus, fend off discouragement. It is particularly important to build a support group of other students and some faculty with whom the process can be shared, including the bad days as well as those moments of discovery. A good advisor recognizes the probability of such times from his own "down" periods doing research and will spend time with his advisees helping them overcome their discouragement.

Central to success is the partnership between a student and an advisor. Each has an important, even critical, role to play. If a student can accept that and, as a true partner, share both success and failure experiences with the advisor, most of the troublesome times can be overcome without serious loss of time.

10

The Defense and Publishing the Results

As the student nears the end of the dissertation writing, there are two matters to plan for. These are the defense of the dissertation and one or more journal articles reporting the results of the research.

Preparation for the Defense of the Dissertation

Requirements vary from university to university, but a common requirement is that the student defend the doctoral dissertation before a committee probably consisting of the advisor, the rest of the committee that has assisted in the dissertation, and two or more outside readers who have not been involved in supervising the dissertation.

If the student has done a good job of writing the first chapter, which explains why the dissertation topic is important, and has done a good job of writing the final chapter, which includes a description of the contribution made by the dissertation, then the task of defending the dissertation will be much easier than if that format is not followed. The examining committee is likely to ask questions such as the following:

- Why did you use that research methodology?

- Why did you analyze the data that way?
- Why didn't you analyze the data differently (for example, by using a specified technique frequently used)?
- It was an obvious extension to do . . . why didn't you do it . . .?

The student has generally been so close to the dissertation topic and has been doing so much writing and editing that he or she may have lost sight of the overall flow of the dissertation. In preparation for the defense, it is often helpful to prepare an outline which can be a short presentation, perhaps fifteen minutes, describing why the problem was important, how it arose, what others have done, the methodology that was followed, the results of the investigation, and the contribution to knowledge from the dissertation. In essence, this is an after-the-fact dissertation proposal format. The student is going back to the questions that needed to be answered before the dissertation was begun. The questions are the same, but the answers can now be precise. The dissertation is complete, so the student should be able to clearly explain the reasons for limitations of scope and for exclusions, such as not undertaking parts of the problem or doing certain types of analysis. Some frequent reasons for limitations and exclusions follow:

- It would have been too time consuming, and the committee advisor agreed that it would be sufficient to do the analysis performed.
- The extension might be interesting, but it was not included in order to keep the dissertation within reasonable scope.
- Preliminary investigations showed the technique was not feasible.

The student should not hesitate to explain the contribution made by the dissertation, but he or she should not try to claim more for it than is really there.

The defense of the dissertation may bring out various suggestions. Then the student must decide whether or not more work should be done or if the dissertation should be changed to reflect the suggestions. Generally, the candidate can rely on his advisor and other committee members with whom he or she has been working to help put suggestions in perspective and to decide what suggestions should be implemented. The following are some examples of suggestions which might come up in the defense session and reasonable responses a candidate might make:

Suggestions or Comments

1. I think you should apply the analysis to the problem and see what results you get.

Possible Responses

a. I will be able to do that, since it does not take much time. I will then present the results to my advisor and the dissertation committee. If you feel it is advisable, I will be happy to include the results in the dissertation.

b. I think that I can do it, but I would prefer not to hold up the dissertation unless you feel that it is necessary for approval. I will, however, do the analysis and, if it is interesting, will include the results in the journal article that I am writing to report the reserch.

c. The analysis sounds interesting, but because of the possible time required to do it and the uncertain

2. I have the following editorial comments:

    a. You state the case too strongly on page 139.

    b. You draw an invalid conclusion from the quotation by Nevert.

results, I would like to handle it as a postdissertation activity.

    a. If the committee is agreeable, I will make the corrections you suggest and will present them to my advisor for approval before the dissertation is sent for final binding.

    b. I tend to disagree with your comment about the conclusions I have drawn because .... I can indicate the alternative view that is taken by others, if that would improve the dissertation.

The candidate should be willing to respond in a positive way to small suggestions, but if suggestions seem to involve a good deal of work, it is well to get the committee to discuss them fully and arrive at a consensus as to what should be done. The candidate should probably summarize, at the end of the dissertation defense, any additions or corrections the committee has requested that he or she make, dividing them into those that must be incorporated in the dissertation before it is finally approved and those comments which involve suggestions that are better handled by future work or future research.

The Journal Article

If the dissertation is a good one, it generally deserves to have the results reported in a scholarly journal. So many students are worn out by the time they complete the dissertation that they never complete the journal article. Only about fifteen percent of the American doctoral dissertations have been reported in a journal article.[1] In order to improve the probability of a journal article from the dissertation, a student should plan for it during the dissertation process. At the time the dissertation is receiving the final reading, there is generally a delay period which the student can profitably use for preparing the journal article. The student should not think that all that is needed is a copy of the dissertation, a pair of scissors, and a couple of hours in order to produce a journal article. The journal article needs to be condensed and the style needs to be slightly different from that of the dissertation. Therefore, the student should allocate perhaps forty to eighty hours to the preparation of the journal article.

When writing the journal article, one approaches it in the same way as writing the dissertation chapter. A detailed outline is prepared to insure that the flow of ideas is correct. The article is written, edited, rewritten, re-edited, and rewritten until an acceptable draft is prepared. An appropriate journal is selected, and the article is sent to the editor in charge of such articles. The student and his or her advisor may wish to have one article prepared for a scholarly journal in the field, but the student may also wish to do a more popular type of article for a magazine having wide readership.

A question which arises is the extent to which the advisor or another member of the committee should be invited to par-

---

[1] Julie L. Moore, "Bibliographic Control of American Doctoral Dissertation," *Special Libraries,* (June 1972): 289.

ticipate in the journal article. In general, courtesy dictates that the advisor should be invited to participate in the journal article. Most advisors have contributed substantially to the quality of a good dissertation and, therefore, they deserve to be asked about being coauthor even though many prefer to let the student do it alone. The ordering of the names in such an article is really not too important. The fact that it is a doctoral dissertation report makes the relationship of the authors quite clear.

The Book

In recent years, less than one percent of doctoral dissertations have been published as books.[2,3] One reason is that many dissertation topics are not suitable as books; another reason is that a dissertation must be rewritten to be publishable as a book. In order to be viable as a regular commercial venture, a book should generally have a well-defined market and a potential five-year sale of 10,000 or more copies. However, a book need not be published by a commercial publisher; there are specialized markets such as university presses or professional organization monograph series. These will publish books written for a smaller, specialized audience.

If you feel your dissertation subject matter is suitable as a text, keep in mind the need for rewriting. A dissertation generally has a fairly rigid structure and uses a scholarly, "academic" prose. A book needs to flow more easily. The dissertation generally has a cautious, formal style with footnotes documenting every significant statement; the book needs a more read-

---

[2]J. L. Moore, "Bibliographic Control," p. 289.

[3]For a description of the differences between a dissertation and a book written from it, *see* Frances G. Halpenny, "The Thesis and the Book," *Press Notes,* (University of Toronto Press, January 1968).

able, confident style, dropping many footnotes. The following are suggestions for revision or rewriting to produce a book:[4]

1. Reduce or eliminate the review of the literature. A summary or background discussion is more suitable in establishing a place for your work.

2. Reduce the number of levels of subdivisions. Use the flow of the text to make the separation of ideas.

3. Reduce repetition. The introduction, analysis, and summary chapters of dissertations often have much overlapping material. The style of dissertation chapters is often repetitious.

4. Eliminate all footnotes which do not add substance. Footnotes which merely support reasonable assertions can frequently be dropped.

5. Rewrite for readability. Short, straightforward sentences without jargon are needed. Read it aloud to identify sentences that need rewriting.

Conclusion

We have traced the successful path of the dissertation from the time it was a suggestion, reflection, or a beginning idea, to its presentation to the professional public in a journal article. We have examined ways to take those interesting ideas and formulate them into researchable hypotheses or problems. The testing of the hypotheses and investigation of important problems have become manageable by planning and systematically approaching what would have been, otherwise, a nebulous and, at times, seemingly impossible task.

---

[4]*See also* David Horne, "Six for Jaffe," *Scholarly Books in America,* VII, no. 4 (April 1965): 2.

We believe that the essence of the approach is the partnership of candidate and advisor; the initiative for planning, preparing, searching and testing must lie with the candidate, while the responsibility for supporting, encouraging, critically evaluating, and suggesting lies with the advisor and the committee. When this partnership is strengthened by the systematic use of the suggestions and approaches offered here, we have found the task not only manageable but quite enjoyable. We hope it will be for you also.

Bibliography

Allen, Don Cameron. *The Ph.D. in English and American Literature.* New York: Holt, Rinehart and Winston, Inc., 1969.

Berelson, Bernard. *Graduate Education in the United States.* New York: McGraw Hill Book Company, 1960.

Chambers, M. M. "Selection, Definition and Delimitation of a Doctoral Research Problem." *Phi Delta Kappan* 42 (3) (1963): 71-73.

Heiss, A. M. *Challenges to Graduate Schools.* San Francisco: Jossey Bass, 1970.

Koefod, Paul Eric. *The Writing Requirements for Graduate Degrees.* Englewood Cliffs, New Jersey: Prentice-Hall, 1964.

Moore, Julie. "Bibliographic Control of American Doctoral Dissertations." *Special Libraries,* July 1972, p. 287.

Rogers, Carl R. *Freedom to Learn.* Columbus, Ohio: Charles E. Merrill Publishing Company, 1969.

Spurr, Stephen H. *Academic Degree Structures: Innovative Approaches.* New York: McGraw Hill Book Company, 1970.

Wilson, Kenneth M. *Of Time and the Doctorate.* Atlanta, Georgia: Southern Regional Education Board Research Monograph 9, 1965.

Selected Tools and Techniques for Searching the Literature

This short appendix cannot describe all of the tools and techniques for searching the literature. It will, however, identify some tools and techniques that are likely to be useful in a search strategy.

Selected Guides to Literature Search

In following a search strategy, it is important to be familiar with guides to library search. A representative list of such guides is included. The dissertation search process is important to dissertation writing, so the references to dissertations are listed separately.

GUIDES TO LIBRARY SOURCES

Brooks, P. C. *Research in Archives: The Use of Unpublished Primary Sources.* Chicago: University of Chicago Press, 1969.

Chandler, G. *How to Find Out.* New York: Pergamon Press, 1974.

Cheney, Frances Heal. *Fundamental Reference Sources.* Chicago: American Library Association, 1971.

Daniells, Lorna. *Business Information Sources.* Berkeley: University of California Press, 1976.

Downs, R. B. *How to Do Library Research.* Urbana, Illinois: University of Illinois Press, 1966.

Galin, S. and P. Spielberg. *Reference Books: How to Select and Use Them.* New York: Random House, 1969.

Gilooly, William B. *The Literature Search.* Somerset, New Jersey: Mariner, 1969.

Jackson, E. *Subject Guide to Major United States Government Publications.* Chicago: American Library Association, 1968.

McInnis, R. G., and J. W. Scott. *Social Science Research Handbook.* New York: Barnes and Noble Books, 1974.

Rogers, A. R. *The Humanities.* Littleton, Colorado: Libraries Unlimited, Inc., 1974.

Schmeckehier, L. F., and R. B. Eastin. *Governmnet Publications and Their Use,* 2nd ed. Washington, D.C.: The Brookings Institution, 1969.

Sheehy, E. P. *Guide to Reference Books.* 9th ed. Chicago: American Library Association, 1976.

United States Government. 1973. *Guide to Government Publications.* 1973. Documents Index, McLean, Virginia. Looseleaf, with quarterly updating.

Walford, Albert John. *Guide to Reference Materials.* 3rd ed. London: Library Association, 1973-1975. Two volumes.

Wasserman, Paul (ed.). *Encyclopedia of Business Information Sources.* Detroit: Gale Research Company, 1976.

White, Carl M. *Sources of Information in the Social Sciences.* Chicago: American Library Association, 1973.

Wynar, Bohdan S. (ed.). *American Reference Books Annual.* Littleton, Colorado: Libraries Unlimited, Inc. 1970.

REFERENCES FOR DISSERTATION SEARCH

American Doctoral Dissertations. Annual listing of dissertations, beginning in 1934 (under slightly different title).

Comprehensive Dissertation Index 1861-1972. Ann Arbor, Michigan 48106 : Xerox University Microfilms .Annual supplements for subsequent years. Lists virtually every doctoral dissertation awarded since American doctoral programs began (417,000 through 1972). A five-volume author index and thirty-two volumes divided by discipline and organized by key words in titles. If the dissertation is abstracted in *Dissertation Abstracts International,* this is referenced.

Dissertation Abstracts International. Ann Arbor, Michigan 48106: Xerox University Microfilms. Abstracts of doctoral dissertations in the United States, Canada, and, since 1975. Europe as well.

Computer Search Services

Two types of search services using computers are available:
1. Organizations that maintain a database and provide search services
2. Organizations, such as universities or computer service bureaus, that use databases provided by data collecting organizations to provide search services.

In using computer search services, the researcher or information specialist must define key words that will be used in the search. The selection of the key words is critical to the success of the search and, therefore, should be done with great care. General terms should never be used without modifiers. For example, a researcher interested in *information systems* would have obtained in a DATRIX search of dissertations (through 1972) 1582 references with *information* in the title and 6520 with *systems* in the title. Only by combining the two words in the search can the search be selective. Most databases have lists of indexing terms for use in formulating search requests.

A useful survey (even though somewhat out of date) of computer-based information service is:

B. Marron, E. Fong, and D. Fife, *A Mechanized Information Services Catalog* (U. S. Government Printing Office, 1974, Catalog Number C13.46:814).

The lists of search services are not intended to be complete; rather, they are examples reflecting the type and scope of such services. The examples tend to include significant and widely used services available in 1977.

EXAMPLES OF SEARCH SERVICES PROVIDED BY DATA COLLECTION ORGANIZATIONS

DATRIX II, Xerox University Microfilms, Ann Arbor, Michigan 48106. DATRIX II is an expansion of the original DATRIX service which includes 99 percent of all doctoral dissertations from 1961 to the present (over one-half million). The search is performed using key words in dissertation titles. The result is a listing of all dissertations having the key words in the titles, plus salient bibliographic data identifying the dissertation. Service is by mail, taking about one week. The basic search fee ($15 in 1978) includes up to 150 references, with a small charge for additional titles.

NAARS, National Automated Accounting Research System. Under the auspices of the American Institute of Certified Public Accountants, 1211 Avenue of the Americas, New York, New York 10036, the NAARS system is a full text interactive search using multiple terms. The database consists of the full text of financial statements—annual reports, prospectuses, accounting policy statements—for companies whose stock is traded on the various stock exchanges. Cost for a single inquiry is about $200. More extensive, individual use may be arranged.

NTISearch, National Technical Information Service (NTIS), Springfield, Virginia 22161. This computer search uses information specialists to formulate requests from customer specifications. File contains abstracts of federally sponsored research, starting from 1964. A number of searches are routinely performed, and results are published at relatively low cost. Custom searches range in cost from $100 to $200. The result of a search is a short abstract and bibliographic data on every report which met the search criteria.

SSIE, The Smithsonian Science Information Exchange, 1730 M Street, N.W., Washington, D.C. 20036. This is a national registry of research in progress. It covers over 100,000 projects in social sciences, behavioral sciences, agriculture sciences, biological sciences, medical sciences, physics, mathematical sciences, materials, electronics and electrical engineering, earth and space sciences, chemistry and chemical engineering, and engineering. Operated by the Smithsonian Institution, custom computer searches are available at a cost of between $50 and $100. Prerun search packages are prepared on specific topics; lists of these search results are published in the "SIEE Science Newsletter."

EXAMPLES OF DATABASES AVAILABLE THROUGH DATA SEARCH AND RETRIEVAL SERVICES

There are (in 1978) a large number of actively maintained databases. For example, one commercial retrieval service provides access to thirty-five databases. The eight listed here are illustrative of the types of databases available for search. Typical cost of a search including a printed list of citations ranges from $15 to $50.

Agricola. Beltsville, Maryland 20705: National Agricultural Library. Lists documents, including journal articles and monographs, in the field of agriculture and related subjects. Begins with 1970.

BIOSIS. Philadelphia, Pennsylvania: Biological Sciences Information Service. Includes contents of *Biological Abstracts,* which contains abstracts of research studies published in over 8,000 journals.

CHEMCON. Columbus, Ohio 43210: Chemical Abstracts Service Division of American Chemical Society. Includes bibliographic references and key word index from *Chemical Abstracts* beginning 1968.

COMPENDEX. New York, New York 10017. Engineering Index, Inc. Is computer file of *Engineering Index* beginning 1969.

ERIC. Bethesda, Maryland 20014: Educational Resources Information Center. Includes abstracts of research and related projects in education beginning with 1965.

Psych Abstracts. Washington, D.C. 20036: American Psychological Association. File contains non-evaluative summaries of world literature in psychology and related disciplines starting 1967. Corresponds to contents of *Psychological Abstracts.*

Sociological Abstracts. Equivalent, for 1963-1971, to the title citations in the printed index in *Sociological Abstracts.* Citations, starting with 1972, also contain abstracts.

Social Scisearch indexes 1,000 social science journals but does not contain abstracts. Starts with 1972. Equivalent printed index is *Social Science Citation Index.*

SUGGESTIONS ON COMPUTER SEARCH FROM RECENT EXPERIENCES

A recent doctoral candidate[1] conducted nine literature searches using ERIC, PSYCH ABSTRACTS, DATRIX, and NTIS search activities. Some suggestions were derived from his experiences.

The candidate combined a manual search of *Comprehensive*

---

[1]A. Milton Jenkins, now Assistant Professor, University of Indiana.

Dissertation Index with the use of DATRIX, which searches the same database. The automated search used 14 key words, combined into 10 different sets of search keys (e.g., INFORMA-TION *AND* SYSTEMS). The results were:

	Total	*Not Relevant*
Manual search of index (and related abstracts)	253	0
Computer search of index	169	37

These results suggest that the automated searches are very useful but cannot do as comprehensive or as complete a search as can be performed manually. A suitable strategy might be to use a computer search as the major search method in areas which are not critical, but use it as a supplement in the most critical areas of literature search.

Almost all of the search systems (DATRIX is a major exception) operate with an information search specialist who assists in formulating the search request. The search requests are generally formulated as sets of search terms combined with the logical (Boolean) operator AND and possibly OR and NOT as well. For example, a complex request might be SYSTEMS AND THEORY NOT GENERAL. This means that the effectiveness of the search depends upon the skill of the specialist and the ability of the researcher to explain the search requirements in a meaningful way.

To improve search effectiveness, a researcher should become familiar with—

1. the contents of the database; including list of publications and rationale for including items;
2. methods of obtaining documents and similar materials, uncovered by the search;
3. the structure and content of the system dictionary of key words or descriptors;

4. the method of constructing search instructions (using key words and logical operators);
5. the likely number of items to be obtained by a search request, sometimes provided by documentation (also obtained through trial searches).

Selected References on Research

There are a large number of references on research methodology, research design, and statistical analysis. A researcher should become familiar with the research methodology in the field of the dissertation. The selected references form a starting point for an extended research methodology review. The list contains no standard, elementary statistics texts, but it does suggest some texts that may be useful in selection of statistical method and more advanced statistical analysis. Also included are dissertation writing guides and style manuals.

Research Approach and Methodology

Boyd, R. D., and M. V. DeVault. "The Observation and Recording of Behavior." *Review of Educational Research* 36 (5) (1966): 529-551.

Burke, Arvid J. and Mary A. Burke. *Documentation in Education.* New York: Teachers College Press, 1967.

Cronbach, L. J. *Essentials of Psychological Testing.* New York: Harper and Row, 1960.

Cronbach, L. J. and G. C. Gleser. *Psychological Tests and Personnel Decisions.* Urbana, Illinois: University of Illinois Press, 1965.

Fishbein, Martin ed. *Readings in Attitude Theory and Measurement.* New York: Wiley, 1967.

Fiske, D. W. *Measuring the Concepts of Personality.* Chicago: Aldine, 1971.

Forcese, Dennis P. and S. Richer, eds. *Stages of Social Research.* Englewood Cliffs, New Jersey: Prentice-Hall, Inc. 1970.

Helmstadter, G. C. *Research Concepts in Human Behavior.* New York: Appleton-Century-Crofts, 1970.

Hyman, H., et al. *Interviewing in Social Research.* Chicago: University of Chicago Press, 1954.

Jackson, Douglas N. and Samuel Messick eds. *Problems in Human Assessment.* New York: McGraw-Hill, 1967.

Kahn, R. L. and C. F. Connell. *The Dynamics of Interviewing.* New York: Wiley, 1957.

Kaplan, Abraham. *The Conduct of Inquiry: Methodology for Behavioral Science.* New York: Chandler Publishing Company, 1964.

Kish, Leslie. *Survey Sampling.* New York: Wiley, 1965.

Market Research Society. *Attitude Scaling.* London: The Oakwood Press, 1960.

Oppenheim, A. N. *Questionnaire Design and Attitude Measurement.* New York: Basic Books, 1966.

Richardson, S. A., B. S. Dohrenwend, and D. Klein. *Interviewing: Its Forms and Functions.* New York: Basic Books, 1965.

Robinson, John P. and Phillip R. Shaver. *Measures of Social Psychological Attitudes.* Ann Arbor, Michigan: Survey Research Center, Institute for Social Research, The University of Michigan, 1969.

Sidman, Murray. *Tactics of Scientific Research.* New York: Basic Books, Inc., 1960.

Setiz, C., M. Johoda, M. Deutsch, and S. W. Cook. *Research Methods in Social Relations.* rev. ed. London: Methuen and Company, 1966. Original edition published by Holt, Rinehart and Winston in 1959.

Strinchcombe, Arthur L. *Constructing Social Theories.* New York: Harcourt, Brace and World, Inc., 1968.

Webb, E. J., D. T. Campbell, R. D. Schwartz, and L. Sechrest. *Unobtrusive Measures: Nonreactive Research in the Social Sciences.* Chicago: Rand McNally, 1966.

Wright H. F. "Observational Child Study." Edited by P. E. Mussen In *Handbook of Research Methods in Child Development,* New York: Wiley, 1960.

Research Design

Brodbeck, May. "Logic and Scientific Method in Research on Teaching." *Handbook of Research on Teaching,* edited by N. L. Gage. Chicago: Rand McNally, 1963.

Campbell, Donald T. and Julian C. Stanley. "Experimental and Quasi-Experimental Design for Research on Teaching." *Handbook of Research on Teaching,* edited by N. L. Gage. Chicago: Rand McNally, 1963. Also published separately as *Experimental and Quasi-Experimental Designs for Research.* Chicago: Rand McNally, 1963.

Cox, D. R. *Planning of Experiments.* New York: John Wiley & Sons, Inc., 1958.

Davitz, Joel R. and Lois Jean Davitz. *A Guide for Evaluating Research Plans in Psychology and Education.* New York: Teachers College Press, 1967.

Elam, S. and J. C. Stanley, eds. *Improving Experimental Design and Statistical Analysis.* Chicago: Rand McNally, 1966.

Evan, W. M., ed. *Organizational Experiments.* New York: Harper and Row, 1971.

Gephart, W. J., R. B. Ingle, and G. Saretsky. *Similarities and Differences in Research and Evaluation Processes.* Bloomington, Indiana: Phi Delta Kappa, 1973.

Glaser, B. G. and A. L. Strauss. *The Discovery of Grounded Theory.* Chicago: Aldine Publishing Company, 1967.

Glock, Charles Y., ed. *Survey Research in the Social Sciences.* New York: Russell Sage Foundation, 1967.

Keppel, Geoffrey. *Design and Analysis: A Researcher's Handbook.* Englewood Cliffs, New Jersey: Prentice-Hall, Inc., 1973. Design and analysis of factorial experiments.

Statistical Analysis

Andrews, F. M., L. Kelm, T. N. Davidson, P. M. O'Malley, and W. L. Rodgers. *A Guide for Selecting Statistical Techniques for Analyzing Social Science Data.* Ann Arbor, Michigan: Survey Research Center, University of Michigan, 1974. Very useful. Recommended.

Blalock, Hubert M., Jr. *Causal Inferences in Nonexperimental Research.* Chapel Hill, North Carolina: The University of North Carolina Press, 1964.

Glass, G. V., V. K. Willson, and J. M. Goltman. *The Design and Analysis of Time Series Experiments.* Boulder, Colorado: Laboratory of Educational Research Press, 1973.

Holtzman, W. H. "Statistical Models for the Study of Change in the Single Case." *Problems in Measuring Change,* edited by C. Harris, Madison, Wisconsin: University of Wisconsin Press, 1963.

Neter, John and William Wasserman. *Applied Linear Statistical Models.* Homewood, Illinois: Richard D. Irwin, Inc., 1974.

Pool, Ithiel de Sola, ed. *Trends in Content Analysis.* Urbana, Illinois: University of Illinois Press, 1959.

Rummel, R. J. *Applied Factor Analysis.* Evanston, Illinois: Northwestern University Press, 1970.

Siegel, Sidney. *Nonparametric Statistics for the Behavioral Sciences.* New York: McGraw-Hill, 1956. Highly regarded reference for nonparametric statistics.

Winkler, Robert L. and William L. Hayes. *Statistics: Probability, Inference, and Decision.* 2nd ed. New York: Holt, Rinehart and Winston, 1975.

Dissertation Writing Guides and Style Manuals

It is important to select a dissertation style early so that all writing is consistent as to headings, references, and other such components. Some universities specify a style to be used; others will accept any reasonable style. A very useful reference for use for selecting words in writing is a thesaurus. Any of the readily available thesauruses should be satisfactory.

Boory, Dorothea M. and Gordon P. Martin. *A Guide to Writing Research Papers.* New York: McGraw-Hill Book Company, 1971.

Campbell, W. G. *Form and Style in Thesis Writing.* Boston: Houghton Mifflin, 1969.

Markman, Roberta and Marie L. Waddell. *10 Steps in Writing the Research Paper.* New York: Barron's Educational Series, Inc., 1971.

Seeber, E. D. *A Style Manual for Students: For the Preparation of Term Papers, Essays and Theses,* Bloomington, Indiana: Indiana University Press, 1967.

The MLA Style Sheet, 2nd ed. The Modern Language Association of America, 1970.

Turabian, K. L. *A Manual for Writers of Term Papers, Theses, and Dissertations.* 4th ed. Chicago: University of Chicago Press, 1973. A very popular style reference.

Using the Computer to Process Analyses of Research Data

The computer may be used in research in a variety of ways. Three major uses are—

1. data reduction and analysis;
2. testing of models and computational procedures;
3. computer as part of research environment, such as computer-assisted instruction.

This appendix will focus on the first use—for data reduction and analysis.

Alternatives for Computer Use

For data reduction and analysis, the researcher may have a choice of a batch processing environment or interactive time-sharing. In using one of these computational environments, the researchers may prepare their own programs or use pre-written programs (termed packages). The appendix will provide some criteria for selecting among alternatives and provide some suggestions for using a package. Many researchers have problems in preparing data on punched cards for batch processing, so a section of the appendix discusses ten questions related to that task.

BATCH VERSUS INTERACTIVE PROCESSING

In the batch method, the researcher submits processing instructions to the computer center, which runs the job and returns printed output. The most common approach to batch job submission is a job deck consisting of a set of punched cards. The data to be processed may be included in the job deck, or the job instructions may specify that the data items to be used are located in a user file on a magnetic tape or on a disk. The job instructions will also specify the program to be used. This program may be—

1. a prewritten program (a package) available from the computer system;
2. a program the user has previously written and stored at the computer center;
3. a program included in the job deck.

In the interactive method, the researcher uses a computer terminal to enter processing instructions and data. The computer program performs the processing immediately and outputs the results on the terminal. The program execution may include a dialogue in which the researcher is asked to select processing options, examine intermediate results, and similar questions. The program to be used may be a package available on the system or a program written (at the terminal) by the researcher.

In general, the batch method is preferred for large data files, extensive outputs, or long processing times. The interactive method is preferred for small data files, limited outputs, and short processing times. Interactive mode is especially useful for situations where selection of processing procedures is done iteratively, based on results being obtained.

OWN PROGRAM VERSUS PACKAGE PROGRAM

Writing a computer program to perform analysis allows the researcher to meet the specific needs of the research project.

The disadvantages are the time and skill requirements to plan, code, and debug (remove errors from) a new program. If a researcher has had no prior experience in computer programming, the writing of a program requires the researcher to learn a programming language. The option of hiring someone to write the program is available but, even in this case, the researcher should have sufficient programming knowledge to supervise and review the programs written.

It requires from ten to forty hours to develop a useful proficiency in a high-level programming language (including writing and debugging a few sample programs). The time estimates for the most commonly used languages are:

FORTRAN	30 - 40 hours
PL/I	40 - 50
BASIC	10 - 15
APL	10 - 15

Time estimates for writing and debugging computer programs depend upon many factors. A major point to keep in mind is that writing instructions probably takes less than thirty percent of the total time to prepare a program. There are several major steps in developing a program. Using four steps in the process, the following estimates may be useful:

Major Steps in Programming	*Estimate of Time*
Problem analysis	Very dependent on problem — say equal to coding time.
Program planning and documentation	One-half of coding time.
Coding of instructions	5 to 10 instructions per hour.
Debugging	Equal to coding time.

These estimates focus on lines of coded instructions. To use the method, a researcher who has not programmed before may need to ask for coded line estimates from experienced programmers.

If the "own program" alternative is selected, a programming language must be chosen. Most analysis programs are written in an algebraic language, but other languages are available for specialized purposes.

Type of Program	Examples of Language to Consider
Analysis	Algebraic
	FORTRAN
	PL/I
	BASIC
	APL
	ALGOL
Simulation	Simulation language
	GPSS
	SIMSCRIPT
	An algebraic language
Text (string) Processing	String processing language
	SNOBOL
	PL/I

As a general rule, select a commonly used language. An algebraic language is generally preferred unless the problem is clearly of a specialized type which can best be programmed by a specialized language. Of the algebraic languages listed, BASIC and APL are used primarily for interactive work. FORTRAN is the most commonly used algebraic language and is available for interactive or batch processing. PL/I and ALGOL have strong advocates but are not used as much as FORTRAN.

The alternative to writing a computer program is to use a pre-written program—a package. The disadvantage of a package is mainly that it may not do exactly what is desired, but the advantages are very persuasive:

1. Packages are fully tested.
2. Packages are generally quite flexible with a number of options.
3. Analysis can be replicated by other researchers using the same package (if generally available).
4. Packages tend to be well documented with instructions for use.
5. Assistance is generally more available with use of a package than with a unique user program.

As a general rule, the researcher should use a package instead of writing a program if the package can provide the processing that is needed.

Selecting a Package Program or Subroutine

There are prewritten programs to do a large number of computational and data processing tasks. For example, most installations have utility programs for such tasks as sorting, and making changes in a file of records. However, for researchers, the most important prewritten programs are mathematics and statistics packages and mathematics and statistics subroutines. Before making decisions about package or subroutine use, the researcher should obtain a list of those that are available on the computer being used.

The processing elements that can be obtained through the package program or sets of subroutines are usually quite extensive, including the following:

1. *Data screening and basic statistics* This includes tabulation, cross tabulation, frequency plots, mean, standard deviation, ranges, and similar data. The screening routines generally allow for data transformations and other coding.

2. *Regression analysis*   Options generally available are simple regression, multiple linear regression, and stepwise regression. Nonlinear regression and polynominal regression may also be included.

3. *Analysis of variance*   The programs will generally provide analysis for all standard experimental designs, such as a completely randomized, randomized complete block, randomized incomplete block, Latin squares, factorial, and so on.

4. *Estimation and hypothesis testing*   These include factor analysis, discriminant analysis, interval estimates of the parameters of various probability density functions, t-tests, and contingency table tests.

5. *Other analysis and processing*   Other analyses include time series analyses and concordance coefficient for agreement of ranks. Other statistical processing requirements may include sorting, matrix arithmetic, and random generation.

STATISTICAL PROGRAM PACKAGES

The statistical program package operates as an independent application. It accepts specifications provided by the user and then performs the specified processing. The user writes no program, only sets of specifications. These instructions must, of course, be in the form required by the package. No knowledge of computer programming is required (although it may be helpful). A few large statistical packages dominate multipurpose processing needs; there are, however, many small, limited-scope packages. There are packages for batch processing and for interactive timesharing. The two most common batch processing packages having wide availability are SPSS and BMD/BMDP.

1. *SPSS (Statistical Package for the Social Sciences)*   This is comprehensive program for processing common to

SPSS Specifications for Descriptive Statistics and Scatter Diagram

Run Name	Income vs. Contributions
File Name	Scatter Analysis of Monthly Income and Consolidated Fund
Variable List	Income, Contrib
Input Medium	Card
N of Cases	70
Input Format	Freefield
Var Labels	Income Monthly Gross Income / Contrib Consolidated Fund
Condescriptive	All
Statistics	All
Read Input Data	
Scattergram	Contrib (0,400) with Income (0,4000)
Options	4, 7
Finish	

Descriptive Statistics Output

Variable Income   Monthly Gross Income

Mean	1321.232	Std Err	155.700	Std Dev	1302.678
Variance	1696971.255	Kurtosis	10.187	Skewness	2.588
Minimum	20.000	Maximum	8252.070	Sum	92486.270
C.V. Pct	98.596	.95 C.I.	1010.620	To	1631.845

Valid Cases   70   Missing Cases   0

Variable Contrib   Consolidated Fund

Mean	101.088	Std Err	14.284	Std Dev	119.512
Variance	13283.146	Kurtosis	16.060	Skewness	3.220
Minimum	1.000	Maximum	814.040	Sum	7076.170
C.V. Pct	118.226	.95 C.I.	72.591	To	129.585

Valid Cases   70   Missing Cases   0

Scatter Diagram Output

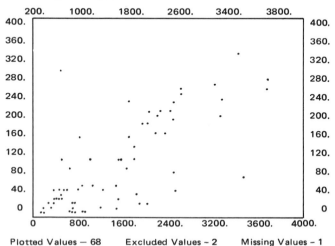

Plotted Values — 68   Excluded Values – 2   Missing Values – 1

III-1. Example of input to SPSS statistical package and resulting outputs.

(reprinted by permission from Gordon B. Davis, Introduction to Computers, 3rd Edition, McGraw-Hill Book Company, New York, 1977, Page 391) social sciences. It is maintained by the National Opinion Research Center, University of Chicago. A manual is available: Norman H. Nie, et al., *Statistical Package for the Social Sciences,* 2nd ed., McGraw-Hill Book Company, New York, 1975. A short manual covering the most common elements is: William R. Klecka, Norman H. Nie, and C. Hadlai Hull, *SPSS Primer,* McGraw-Hill Book Company, 1975.

2. *BMDP and BMD (Biomedical Computer Programs)*[1] Assembled and maintained by the Health Sciences Computer Facility at the University of California at Los Angeles, the newer BMDP contains twenty-six programs, while BMD contains over fifty programs. These have wide use. *BMD Biomedical Computer Programs,* University of California Press, 1973; *BMDP Biomedical Computer Programs,* University of California Press, 1975.

The simplicity and ease of use of the statistical packages is illustrated by an example. Figure III-1 is a sample of specification input and resultant output for an SPSS program. The data consists of seventy pairs of data items for monthly gross income and amounts contributed to the Consolidated Fund drive. The specifications call for descriptive statistics and a scattergram (in which two extreme values were eliminated).

There are a large number of small packages for interactive use. The most widely used large package is OMNITAB II. This is a large, unified set of computer routines developed by the National Bureau of Standards to do statistical and numerical analysis. It is available from the National Technical Information Service (NTIS), 5285 Port Royal Road, Springfield, Virginia 22161. A manual is available: *OMNITAB II Users Reference*

---

[1] For a comparison of BMD and BMDP programs, see James W. Frane, "The BMD and BMDP Series of Statistical Programs," *Communications of the ACM,* October 1976, pp. 570-576.

Manual, U. S. Government Printing Office, October, 1971, 253 pages.

MATHEMATICAL AND STATISTICAL SUBROUTINES

Mathematical and statistical subroutines are available for use in a program written in a high-level language (such as FORTRAN or PL/I). In other words, the researcher writes a program (for example, in FORTRAN) and inserts in the program a statement which uses the subroutine (instead of the researcher doing that part of the program coding). For example, a researcher desiring to perform a Kolmogorov-Smirnov test of two samples to test the hypothesis of equality of distributions from which the two samples are taken[2] could write a FORTRAN program consisting of the following:

1. Statements to read data for the two samples
2. Statements to validate data
3. Statements to print input data for visual inspection
4. Statements (or a call to a subroutine) to sort each sample into ascending order
5. A statement to call the Kolmogorov-Smirnov subroutine, for example (using the IMSL subroutines): CALL NKS2 (F,N,G, M,PDIF,IER)

   (The six names inside the parentheses are replaced by names defined by the programmer. The names replacing F and G refer to the two samples, and names replacing N and M refer to the sample sizes. The name assigned to the position of PDIF is a six position array to hold six parts of the result. The last name in the call is the name assigned to hold error codes.)

---

[2] This test might be used on the samples of dissertation lengths presented in Figure 2-1 to test the hypothesis that the underlying distributions are equal, i.e., the distribution of page lengths is the same for the fields sampled.

6. Statements to print a report (including results from sub-routine stored in the result array)

Almost every computer center has subroutines readily available. Some examples of the subroutines available illustrate their capabilities:

Major category	Example
Analysis of experimental data	Covariance analysis test
Basic statistics	Calculate means, standard deviations, and correlation coefficients
Eigen analysis	Eigenvalues and eigenvectors of a symmetric matrix
Random numbers	Generate normal deviates
Nonparametric statistics	Kendall's test for correlation
Sampling	Simple random sampling with continuous data
Vector-matrix arithmetic	Transpose product of matrix

The two most common large subroutine libraries are IMSL and SSP.

1. *IMSL FORTRAN Subroutines* A set of about 200 FORTRAN callable subroutines has been developed and is maintained by International Mathematics and Statistical Libraries, Inc. A manual is available from IMSL. A computing center with this set of subroutines will have documentation available to users.

2. *SSP (Scientific Subroutine Package)* This set of over 200 mathematical and statistical routines is provided by IBM in FORTRAN or PL/I and is available on most IBM equipment and some non-IBM equipment. A manual is available from the IBM Corporation.

Other subroutine packages are also available. For example, IBM has a package of subroutines, designed for forecasting, called the Forecasting And Modeling System (FAMS), and a National Science Foundation project developed a set of FORTRAN routines for eigenvalue and eigenvector computation called EISPACK.

CONSIDERATIONS IN SELECTING A PACKAGE OR SUBROUTINE

At large computer centers, there will be a variety of packages. For example, SPSS and BMD packages and subroutines will be available. The following are considerations in selection:

1. *Package versus Subroutine*
   a. *Type of processing*   If the processing is standard, a package is probably preferred.
   b. *Programming knowledge of user*   Subroutines require programming skill; packages do not.
   c. *Specialized requirements*   Subroutines are preferred because the subroutines can be obtained with unique-need coding.
   d. *Availability of required processing*   Some elements are available in subroutines that are not available in packages.
2. *Selection among Packages or Sets of Subroutines*
   a. *General availability to other researchers*   If research is to be published and subject to replication, a widely available source of computation is preferred.
   b. *Availability of required processing*   All packages have basic statistics, but they differ in coverage for less common analysis.
   c. *Availability of assistance*   Some packages and subroutine libraries are well supported with manuals, consultants, and other necessary materials. Others

are poorly supported. Installation support is not generally the same for all.

References on the Use of Computer

Frane, James W. 1976. The BMD and BMDP Series of Statistical Computer Programs. *Communications of the ACM,* vol. 19, no. 10: 570-576. A useful discussion of the difference between the BMD programs and the newer BMPD programs.

Schucany, W. R.; P. D. Minton; and B. S. Shannon, Jr. 1972. A Survey of Statistical Packages. *Computing Surveys,* vol. 4, no. 2: 64-79. Somewhat out-of-date but still a useful survey.

Slysz, W. D. 1974. An Evaluation of Statistical Software in the Social Sciences. *Communications of the ACM,* vol. 17, no.6: 326-332.

There are so many programming language manuals for algebraic languages (over 100 for the major alegbraic languages) that is is not useful to list them. If the researcher is learning the language in self-study mode, there are manuals that are designed for that purpose. A FORTRAN test that is suitable for self-study and that emphasizes a disciplined, readable style is Gordon B. Davis and Thomas R. Hoffman, *FORTRAN: A Structured, Disciplined Style* (New York: McGraw Hill Book Company, 1978). The style recommended in this reference is especially useful for programs that are to be published in dissertations.

Data Preparation Considerations when Using Punched Cards

A new researcher frequently has very little basis for estimating the cost of keypunching the data. As a rough guide, the following estimation methods may be useful:

1. Calculate number of characters in each set of data (questionnaire, data collection document, etc.).
2. Multiply by number of sets of data to obtain total keystrokes.
3. Divide total keystrokes by 5000 to arrive at number of hours of keypunching (modify this figure by an allowance for document handling, legibility problems, poor data document design, etc.).
4. Multiply hours arrived at in step 3 by rate per hour (including overhead).
5. Repeat above steps for all data items to be key verified.

The design of procedures for keypunching data into cards is important for very lage sets of data. But even small keypunching volumes can benefit from the ten questions in this section.

QUESTIONS ON USE OF COMPUTER

QUESTION	*COMMENTS*
1. Have you reviewed the design of the data collection form with the keypunch service you intend to use?	1. Upon review of the data form from which keypunching will be done, keypuncher will often spot difficulties and provide suggestions for improvement.
2. Can data be punched sequentially as the data form is read, without jumping back and forth?	2. The data should be punched in the same order that it appears on the form. A keypuncher should not be quired to thumb through the data collection document to find the next data item.
3. Are the data items clearly identified on the data form?	3. The data should be clearly marked with lines, boxes, and circles. In some cases, it may be necessary to first edit the data to add codes, circle items to be punched, and so on.

QUESTION

4. Have you checked the input data formatting options available with the analysis package you intend to use (if applicable)?

5. Is it clear where punching of each data item begins on the punched card:
   a. By a column identification for each fixed field size;
   b. By field separators for a free format approach?

6. Does each punched card clearly identify:
   a. The data form from which it came;
   b. The set to which it belongs and the sequence in the set (for multiple card set from a data form)?

COMMENTS

4. Statistical and other analysis packages generally offer several options for ways in which data may be formatted. It is well worth the trouble to check out these options before designing the data collection form.

5. There are essentially two methods for identifying data items on the card.
   a. Each data item is put into a fixed field on the card. For example, "income is punched into columns 20 to 28." Decimal points are required unless the digits are aligned in the field according to digit position.
   b. There is a separator between data items — usually a comma or a space. The data items appear in a defined order. If a data item is missing there will normally be a method of indicating this.

6. All data collection should be given some identification. This identification can be a code assigned to the object of collection, a numerical identifier for the data collection document, and so on. This identifier should be in each card that is punched from the document, in the same position in each card. For example, columns 1 to 5 of every card might be used for the identifier of the document from which it was punched. If there are several cards for the form, another column should be used, for example, column 6, for the sequence number 1, 2, 3). If the number of cards can be varible, then the last card in the set should be given a special code to indicate that there are no more cards in the set.

QUESTION	*COMMENTS*
7. Have you provided for verification— visually proofreading and/or mechanical verification?	7. All keypunching should be verified either mechanically or visually, or both. Mechanical verification essentially doubles the cost of keypunching, but is often worth it, especially for large volumes of data. The researcher should do visual verification even if there has been mechanical verification. It is often easier to use a listing of the cards in visual verification.
8. Have you provided for validation of correctness of data by visual validation and/or special validation program analysis?	8. Validation is provided to check that the data is correct or, at least, reasonably correct. This can be done by visual inspection by the researcher, or a validation program may be written to test data items to make sure they fall within an acceptable range and that there is consistency among data items.
9. Have you created a magnetic tape (or other magnetic storage) for large data volume (over 500 cards) for processing efficiency?	9. For large volumes of data, it is much more efficient to put the data onto magnetic tape or other magnetic storage. This is especially true if the data will be used repeatedly, since each handling of the cards presents an opportunity for the cards to be dropped or damaged, and card reading is less efficient than reading magnetic media.
10. Have you provided a backup, either by a second set of cards or a magnetic tape copy?	10. Cards may be lost or dropped, therefore, it is a wise procedure to create some sort of recovery system. Transcribing to magnetic tape is one method. The cards are then saved as backup. If no tape is made, the cards may be reproduced to provide a backup deck.

No One Can Build Your Writing Skills Better Than We Can...

Essentials of English, 4th Edition
$7.95, Can. $10.95 (4378-2)
The comprehensive program for effective writing skills.

Essentials of Writing, 4th Edition
$8.95, Can. $11.95 (4630-7)
A companion workbook for the material in *Essentials of English.*

10 Steps in Writing the Research Paper, 4th Edition
$7.95, Can. $10.95 (4151-8)
The easy step-by-step guide for writing research papers. It includes a section on how to avoid plagiarism.

How to Write Themes and Term Papers, 3rd Edition
$7.95, Can. $10.95 (4268-9)
The perfect, logical approach to handling theme projects.

The Art of Styling Sentences: 20 Patterns to Success, 2nd Edition
$6.95, Can. $9.95 (2269-6)
How to write with flair, imagination and clarity, by imitating 20 sentence patterns and variations.

Writing The Easy Way,
2nd Edition *$9.95, Can. $13.95 (4615-3)*
The quick and convenient way to enhance writing skills.

Basic Word List, 2nd Edition
$5.50, Can. $7.50 (4377-4)
More than 2,000 words that are found on the most recent major standardized tests are thoroughly reviewed.

BARRON'S EDUCATIONAL SERIES, INC.
250 Wireless Boulevard • Hauppauge, New York 11788
In Canada: Georgetown Book Warehouse
34 Armstrong Avenue • Georgetown, Ontario L7G 4R9

Prices subject to change without notice. Books may be purchased at your bookstore, or by mail from Barron's. Enclose check or money order for total amount plus sales tax where applicable and 10% for postage and handling (minimum charge $1.75, Can. $2.00). All books are paperback editions.
ISBN PREFIX: 0-8120

More selected BARRON'S titles:

DICTIONARY OF ACCOUNTING TERMS
Siegel and Shim
Nearly 2500 terms related to accounting are defined.
Paperback, $9.95, Can. $13.95 (3766-9)

DICTIONARY OF ADVERTISING AND DIRECT MAIL TERMS
Imber and Toffler
Nearly 3000 terms used in the ad industry are defined.
Paperback, $9.95, Can. $13.95 (3765-0)

DICTIONARY OF BANKING TERMS
Fitch
Nearly 3000 terms related to banking, finance and money management.
Paperback, $9.95, Can. $13.95 (3946-7)

DICTIONARY OF BUSINESS TERMS
Friedman, general editor
Over 6000 entries define business terms.
Paperback, $9.95, Can. $13.95 (3775-8)

BARRON'S BUSINESS REVIEW SERIES
These guides explain topics covered in a college-level business course.
Each book: paperback

ACCOUNTING, 2nd EDITION. *Eisen.* $11.95, Can. $15.95 (4375-8)
BUSINESS LAW, *Hardwicke and Emerson.* $11.95, Can. $15.95 (3495-3)
BUSINESS STATISTICS, *Downing and Clark.* $11.95, Can. $15.95 (3576-3)
ECONOMICS, *Wessels.* $10.95, Can. $14.95 (3560-7)
FINANCE, 2nd EDITION. *Groppelli and Nikbakht.* $11.95, Can. $15.95 (4373-1)
MANAGEMENT, *Montana and Charnov.* $10.95, Can. $14.95 (3559-3)
MARKETING, *Sandhusen.* $10.95, Can. $14.95 (3494-5)
QUANTITATIVE METHODS, *Downing and Clark.* $10.95, Can. $14.95 (3947-5)

TALKING BUSINESS SERIES: BILINGUAL DICTIONARIES
Five bilingual dictionaries translate about 3000 terms not found in most foreign phrasebooks.
Each book: paperback

TALKING BUSINESS IN FRENCH, *Le Gal.* $9.95, Can. $13.95 (3745-6)
TALKING BUSINESS IN GERMAN, *Strutz.* $8.95, Can. $11.95 (3747-2)
TALKING BUSINESS IN ITALIAN, *Rakus.* $6.95, Can. $9.95 (3754-5)
TALKING BUSINESS IN JAPANESE, C. *Akiyama and N. Akiyama.* $8.95, Can. $11.95 (3848-7)
TALKING BUSINESS IN KOREAN, *Cheong.* $8.95, Can. $11.95 (3992-0)
TALKING BUSINESS IN SPANISH, *Fryer and Faria.* $9.95, Can. $13.95 (3769-3)

All prices are in U.S. and Canadian dollars and subject to change without notice.
At your bookseller, or order direct adding 10% postage (minimum charge $1.75, Canada $2.00), N.Y. residents add sales tax.   ISBN PREFIX: 0-8120

Barron's Educational Series, Inc.
250 Wireless Boulevard, Hauppauge, NY 11788
Call toll-free: 1-800-645-3476, in NY 1-800-257-5729
In Canada: Georgetown Book Warehouse
34 Armstrong Ave., Georgetown, Ontario L7G 4R9
Call toll-free: 1-800-247-7160

DISSERTATION MANAGEMENT CHECKLIST

		STATUS		PLAN	
	Described in Chapter	Not for me	Done	Will do	Done
1. Early selection of general area for dissertation research	4				
2. Early (or tentative) selection of advisor and committee supportive of probable dissertation area	4				
3. Coursework designed to support probable dissertation area	4				
4. Setting up of dissertation ideas file	4				
5. Familiarity with library research tools available at my school in my area of interest	Appendix I				
6. Familiarity with computer search tools available for my area of interest	Appendix I				
7. Identification of several possible topics	5				
8. Exploratory search of literature and prior research on possible topics	Appendix I				
9. Preparation of several topic analyses	6				
10. Evaluation of topics with advisor (and perhaps committee)	5				
11. Selection of a topic and preparation of a proposal	5				
12. Refining of proposal until accepted	6				
13. Proposal defense (or committee review) to arrive at understanding that if research defined in proposal is done in a scholarly, workmanlike way and written up in suitable dissertation form, it will be accepted	6				
14. Preparation of time schedule	7				
15. Review of critical dates with advisor	8				
16. Establishment of research log or journal and research document filing system	9				
17. Establishment of backup file for all drafts of chapters	9				
18. Use of communication/documentation methods — Report of committee meeting — Note summarizing significant discussion — Agenda for meeting of committee	8				
19. Use of aids to advisor/committee review of drafts — Transmittal memo — Issue summary — Chapter outlines	8				
20. Journal article(s) planned and outlined	10				
21. Defense completed (congratulations!)					